Live Intentional

Live the life you always wanted but never believed you could

VICKI COFFMAN

ISBN 979-8-88540-834-9 (paperback)
ISBN 979-8-88540-835-6 (digital)

Christian Faith Publishing
832 Park Avenue
Meadville, PA 16335
www.christianfaithpublishing.com

Scripture references are from two translations:

Printed in the United States of America

CONTENTS

INTRODUCTION

We have become a world torn asunder. As a society, we are the most rude, crude, and downright abusive people toward each other. We make decisions to criticize and physically assault those who oppose us rather than have a discussion, with intention to find clarity and compromise. When we don't get our way or are challenged in our thinking, we don't know how to think independently, so we speak the rhetoric we've heard and defend it. We never consider that what we believe is a lie because we surround ourselves with similar-thinking people who validate what we think, believe what we believe, and encourage our impulsive, out-of-control behaviors. We have become a society of whiny crybabies who stomp our feet, clench our fists, and blame others instead of taking responsibility for ourselves.

We hate those who succeed. We are jealous of those who are successful because most of us aren't successful. In many situations, individuals and people groups don't have access to the privileges seen all around us, which often delivers unearned success to many who have not had to work for their rewards. Some successes are handed down through familial generations (old money), and the beneficiaries never had to earn a living. Corporate powers deem who is worthy and who is not and promote according to their personal bias and preferences (discrimination). Funding of projects often results in personal gain to the donor (influence). Some people find they must forfeit themselves to succeed (quid pro quo), while others sell their soul to the highest bidder. Paradigms shift. Perspectives prevail, and those who are unsuccessful deem they are unable to become successful because of the barriers they cannot seem to overcome. The results are, we despise those who have what we don't have and minimize their struggle as not hard work but *privilege.*

We hate ourselves. We cut our legs and arms, shoot up illegal street drugs, smoke whatever will burn, and drink whatever is readily available. We have become consumers of the fast and easy in everything in life. We seek comfort above all else, even when to be comfortable means to stop living. We hide in fear of the unknown, fearful of being alone, yet choose to isolate and connect only through technology. We live by our feelings and avoid facts. We confuse lust with love and impulsivity with passion and elevate our own worth by devaluing others.

For many decades, we have been told to not think independently. Social media moguls created algorithms designed to turn one group of people against another. Each group was "fed" misinformation and lies designed to manipulate individuals into believing they were part of a larger group. More and more "friends" voiced similar concerns and accusations of wrongdoing against the identified enemy. Mass delusional psychosis, also known as "groupthink" resulted as groups defined themselves as "social justice warriors" intent on destroying the enemy they were manipulated to hate. There is a false sense of security when everyone thinks, speaks, and acts the same. When others challenge our beliefs, collectively, we can push back and defend what we do. Sadly, all this does not create a true sense of security as the lies increase, stories change, and we're left spinning out of control. Our reliance on our feelings as facts leads us to feel more anxious as we are destabilized emotionally. We lose our peace as frustration pours into our minds. Those who have consistently tried to tell us the truth are the enemy and those who lie to us have abandoned us. We find ourselves alone, helpless, and hopeless. Depression sets in as we realize the parade has left us and taken with them not only the sense of community but everything that gave us passion and purpose.

How do you change this? By learning how to live intentionally. You must find your own path, resist the crowd, and press on even when you fear being alone. You must build faith, seek freedom, and collaborate with others who have gone before you. You must first learn to trust yourself and resist trusting everyone else. You must set your sails against the winds and determine the course for your life. The journey to change is lifelong. It is difficult but very rewarding. You must stop being dependent on others and learn to be independent. The good news is God is waiting for you to guide you, to take your hand and give you community. God believes in you, knows you, and is able to build your faith. If you are ready to live your best life, the life God intended for you to live, then you must learn to live intentional.

CHAPTER 1

Intentional Life

*Therefore, everyone who hears these words
of mine and puts them into practice is like a wise
man who built his house on the rock.*
—Matthew 7:24 (NIV)

Stop complaining. If you want to live a life that is intentional, you must first stop complaining. I understand; truly I do. Life has thrown you some pretty hard challenges, and the struggle has been real. I get it. Life can suck sometimes, but I want to congratulate you that you've made it through those struggles and were smart enough to pick up this book, so there is still hope. Yes, there is always hope as long as you are breathing and open to consider the possibilities. You have undiscovered abilities that are waiting to be developed, skills that you've never learned, and a pathway to success you have never seen before. All these things are within the pages of this book waiting for you to explore. Your life is not defined by your past unless you give power to it. When you determine to look forward to new opportunity and not behind at the limitations, everything is possible. The things you've experienced in your life to this point, the pain and the suffering, pleasure and love, have contributed to who you are today. Those difficulties you experienced, both highs and lows, were building muscles for the weight you had to carry. The more challenges you overcame, the stronger your resolve becomes. If you are tired of the

1

struggle, take heart. Courage is on the other side of fear. The good news is you've already done the really hard work.

Look at each challenge as a gift instead of a hinderance that keeps you sitting in the soup of discouragement. Consider the struggles that prepared you to come to where you are. There may have been times when you were unsure you would have even lived through them. Those moments in time have prepared you for this moment when you can now achieve your true purpose in life. The future awaits you, and you can go through it, or you can grow through it by living intentional.

What does it mean to live an intentional life? Here are some questions you may have considered:

- Can I live intentionally in one part and not so intentional in other areas of my life?
- Can I think I am living intentional only to learn later I was deceived?
- Can I learn how to live intentional even if there is more life behind me than before me?
- Can I teach intentionality to my children and help them make better choices?
- Can I be intentional at work?
- Can I be intentional in a relationship and effect change in another?
- Can I learn to be intentional in my finances even when debt is out of control?

The answer to all these questions is "Yes, you can!"

In considering the topics of this book, I thought long and hard at what are the most common areas people are most often asking for help. The list was extensive, so I compiled them into themes, and those themes are contained in this book. Some of the challenges people face when we are trying to live intentionally have to do with internal forces that impact how we see ourselves. Some areas of concern have to do with how others see us. There are many perspectives in life: how we see ourselves in our environment, our society, and our relationships and how we see ourselves in our faith or lack thereof. Sometimes those perceptions are changed gradually, and in other times, such as in my life, perspectives change suddenly.

When I was eleven years old, I had already suffered more than any little girl should have to suffer. When I was three months old, my mother tried to quiet my crying by throwing me against a wall. Suffice to say, things only got worse from there. The challenges of my youth prepared me for the struggles I would experience as an adult. At the age of eleven, I determined my purpose in life was to become a police officer who could rescue other little boys and girls from harm. For twenty-five years, I lived my purpose to protect and to serve but learned I couldn't save those who would not save themselves. No matter how many times I rescued, I would have to continue to rescue them as they returned to only what they knew.

When I was injured on the job and forced into an unexpected early retirement, I understood their plight as I lost myself in my own despair. At forty-six years old, I found myself unemployed, living on half my income, consumed by debt, and raising a teenager all by myself. I had lost the use of my right hand and had limited use of my left hand. I was riddled in pain from my head to my toes, and any movement sent agonizing shockwaves through my body. The only thing I could do about the pain was cry and scream in agony. The doctors had tried everything from nerve blocks to acupuncture trying to relieve my pain. When the doctors gave up on me, I found myself standing before the psychiatrist assigned to my case. He was compassionate as he said the only thing left was to prescribe me antidepressants. Defeated, I went home and began taking the pills, and they did stop the tears, but they stopped all feelings altogether. I resolved myself to never feel joy again.

One day, I was complaining to a friend that I was so sick and tired of the many limitations I now had to deal with—the way I walked around like a zombie, the way my daughter looked at me with pity, and how I felt empty without any emotions or feelings I hadn't felt in a while.

My friend pointed out something so obvious to her and something I was blind to when she asked me, "Why are you complaining?

When you had time, you didn't have money. When you had money, you didn't have time. Now you have both. Stop complaining and enjoy the blessings you have."

Later that night, while contemplating my friend's words, I suddenly felt feelings and realized I was pissed! I raised my fist and screamed at God. I threw myself to the floor and forced the pain upon me. I screamed more, stomped more, and pounded my fists against the wall. When I was done with my temper tantrum, I noticed something: the pain was the same during the tantrum as it was the rest of the time. Something clicked in my mind as I realized I did not have to let the pain limit me. Either way, living or simply existing, the pain was the same. So that day, I decided right then to stop complaining and start living. That decision meant I had to reinvent myself and find a new purpose. From that moment forward, I began to live intentional.

I quit taking the antidepressants and instead of the dark sadness that enveloped me, I became determined to find a way to live again. I went to the physical therapist who had been gently trying to recover the use of my hand, and I told her I wanted her to hurt me. She looked at me in shock as I told her I wanted her to press upon me the ways to strengthen my muscles and to ignore my pain. I did push-ups, pull-ups, ran, and did weights. I sweated profusely as I cried in unrelenting pain. Soaked and exhausted, I would go home and collapse, all the while feeling like I had been electrocuted. But after months of agony, I found myself getting stronger, leaner, and the tears had stopped. I began to realize that the pain was easing, and my recoveries were shorter. Each day brought a new discovery as I took a fresh look at myself and saw the person I was before the injury. I had lost weight, my eyes were clear, and the color was back in my cheeks. I reconnected with friends I had avoided and reengaged with my daughter again. I found I could laugh, and joy had found its way back to my heart. My circumstances had not changed as I still had pain, but I was able to tolerate it now. I had other concerns about how to press forward without a job and no prospects for my future, but instead of being frozen in fear, I had found myself, and that gave me hope.

Vision

One component of intentionality is *vision*. We can clearly see where we've been, and we can judge ourselves harshly by our mistakes and failures. We can even see where those errors in judgment have brought us to today. All we have to do is look at the damage we've caused in our lives to have evidence to support our beliefs. And we can take those judgments and project them into our future and see the failure that awaits. So we manifest what we believe and create evidence against us that further condemns us to a prison of our own making.

When we have no vision, we must rely on others to provide for us the things we don't have. We subconsciously will seek to confirm and not contradict what we already know about ourselves. If we believe we can't, we won't. We can be afraid of failing, but we can be equally afraid of succeeding as well. Our lack of vision may keep us so fearful of the unknown that we would rather stay where we are—comfortably miserable.

Sometimes we may have a vision or a dream that we wish we could pursue, and we take a step or two in the direction of hope, only to let our insecurities stop us. We may have a blurred vision that prevents us from seeing clearly what is before us and fear we may stumble and fall. We can see but need help finding a path to walk. Fear of rejection and judgment from others can keep us from asking for help and keeps us stuck where we are.

We also may stay where we are because we have vision to see but fear the unknown beyond what is before us. There may be obstacles in our field of view that limit our vision to only where we are and maybe just a little beyond. We are not afraid of failure but question who will we have become when we succeed. We may step only so far as our vision will guarantee, but we will stop when something we value is at risk. Many people forfeit something better that may improve their life, lifestyle, or make them different from their friends, so they forfeit the opportunity rather than risk the potential for loss. This is the saddest of all three reasons why people stay stuck because they can, but they won't.

When we have a clear vision of where we want to go and are determined to arrive at the destination we desire, it's much easier to see our way forward. When we walk toward our destination, even when it is far from view, we are moving with intent. The more intentional we are moving forward, the more confident we become. This confidence builds momentum, and soon you may find yourself running toward your destiny.

Help

Staying on the road you choose requires focused intent as the road may change, the light may dim, and others may not want you to succeed. When we let others pull or push us away from our goals, we end up in places and situations we never intended to be. There is a time to stray from your path when you have a desire to help someone in need. In the Bible, there is a story about one such road and three people who journeyed on it. Jesus explains through a parable how people who live intentionally can do better when they leave their path to help others. And consequently, they are rewarded with more than they expected when they return to the road they left.

Jesus said: "A man was going down from Jerusalem to Jericho, when he was attacked by robbers. They stripped him of his clothes, beat him and went away, leaving him half dead. A priest happened to be going down the same road, and when he saw the man, he passed by on the other side. So too, a Levite, when he came to the place and saw him, passed by on the other side. But a Samaritan, as he traveled, came where the man was; and when he saw him, he took pity on him. He went to him and bandaged his wounds, pouring on oil and wine. Then he put the man on his own donkey, brought him to an inn and took care of him. The next day he took out two denarii and gave them to the innkeeper. 'Look after him,' he said, 'and when I return, I will reimburse you for any extra expense you may have.'

Which of these three do you think was a neighbor to the man who fell into the hands of robbers?"

The expert in the law replied, "The one who had mercy on him."

Jesus told him, "Go and do likewise." (Luke 10:30–37 NIV)

Jesus teaches us that we all have a path to follow that God has laid before us. He does not teach us to blast past others who have fallen or who were attacked while on the road they journeyed. It is our duty to help others who are trying to reach their destination, especially if we are all going the same direction. When mercy is given to another by us, we also can expect to receive mercy from God. To bless others is to bless ourselves.

God creates everyone uniquely. Not everyone has the same gifts or talents as everyone else. It's our uniqueness that makes us special and brings different degrees of success. Those who have not found their unique potential may not be as successful as others, but it is not due to limitations others have placed on them. It is because they have not found or developed their particular gifting or skill to its full potential.

If someone wants to be successful at a career, education, or as a parent, they must work just as hard as a professional athlete in order to become successful. The only difference is the money and fame may not compare. You won't get free clothes or a shoe named after you. You won't have interviews on TV or have your story listed in search engines. But the changes your coworkers, employers, educators, and families see will not go unnoticed. To your spouse and your children, you will be legendary if you work hard to be your best self. Everyone has unique potential, but it will remain your unrealized potential, unless you work to develop it. You determine your level of success, not anyone else. No one can keep you down if you want to soar for the clouds. If you believe and pursue your vision, you just might reach, and maybe even exceed, your unique potential.

Truth

As a person who enjoys absolutes, I like to keep my feet rooted in truth and fact. When the truth is bent toward the motivations of another, it's no longer the foundational truth but a variation of the truth. If you plant an apple seed in the ground, water, and tend it, the seed will produce over time an apple tree. It does not produce a watermelon. Having said that, there are new fruits and vegetables being produced by manipulation of the original fruit or vegetable. Variations of roses have been "created" by merging (grafting) two variations of rose to create a third. People can change, merge, and evolve as well to become a better version of themselves or to become someone completely different from the original.

When you know the truth about who you are, what you believe, and that belief is supported by evidence, you can live with confidence. Truth never changes to become a lie. The truth cannot be a lie and remain the truth. The truth is one of those absolutes that does not evolve. Opinion evolves, and interpretation of the original truth may change, but the truth is, the truth is the truth.

Recently, I spoke with a woman who has made strides to move from victim to victor. She has shared her life challenges with me, which have included some of the most horrific injustices that anyone should never have to experience. Throughout her lifetime, she was told to be quiet, to ignore the truth, and settle for living the lies those others demanded of her for their own protection. Now she has found her voice, is speaking the truth, and is standing up against the injustice she has experienced. She has found her passion and now has fearlessly entered the battle to protect others. She has become a *social justice warrior* and is ready to fight. The pain she has suffered and overcome has prepared her to follow her newfound purpose. The scars of her past no longer hold her back as they have become her badges of honor.

According to *Wikipedia*, "Social justice warrior (SJW) is a pejorative term used for an individual who promotes socially progressive, left-wing, and liberal views, including feminism, civil rights, gay and transgender rights, identity politics and multiculturalism." The accusation that somebody is an SJW carries implications that they are pursuing personal validation rather than any deep-seated conviction and engaging in disingenuous arguments.

I disagree that to be a social justice warrior you must have a particular political lean. Justice is rooted in truth, not politics. Anyone, no matter what their political stance, can be a warrior for social justice—it just depends on which side of the truth you stand. There are those who make claim that they are in the battle, but they are not in the fight. They are the ones who scream and incite others to do the fighting for them while they take the fame and fortune. There are others who put life and limb in harm's way and never receive any credit at all. They are everyday soldiers who leave one battle only to be drawn into another, always defending the weak, the needy, and the broken.

Everyone is fighting one battle or another at any given time. There are so many injustices in the world today you can't help but feel the tension in the air. All you have to do is pick one topic from the extensive list of wrongs and, boom, you're defending yourself, others, or the things you believe. You can fight a battle across your city, your state, or beyond the borders of your country. You can fight against the fear and shame of cultural shifts, and you can fight for the truth. You can fight for honorable things like helping the weak, broken, and vulnerable, and you can fight for the children. You can fight for your job, and you can fight for your freedom. You can fight to protect what is right, and you can fight for what is profitable. You can fight for a particular people group, and you can fight for a nation. You can fight for a stranger, and you can fight for your family.

Once you realize what your battle is and decide to enter the fight, it's amazing how much you are willing to sacrifice. Consider the cost before you enter the fight. Make sure you fight for justice, what is right, honorable, and true, and even if the battle is lost, you will always be on the winning side.

What does it mean to live intentionally? I believe it starts with the truth—the truth of who you are. Challenge the lies you've been told and speak the truth without apologizing for things others have done to you against your will.

I have found that many of the reasons why women and men apologize are rooted in their upbringing. Many were made prisoners who suffered the consequences placed on them by others. Victims of abuse get used to apologizing early in life as they attempt to sidestep the physical, emotional, and sexual abuse from their captors. Even after their abuser is long gone, they tend to fall into relationships that are abusive, and the pattern continues. They have not learned to live a life of intention but, instead, live lives reactive to their environment. They wonder why things happen to them and have no idea how to create the life they desire.

As a therapist, I counsel my clients to stop living their life as if they have no choice in the outcome. You have power, you have control, and you have the choice to walk away from the patterns that keep you prisoner. If you are sick and tired of being walked on, leave. If you are exhausted being responsible for another's choices, stop. If you are fearful of the unknown, find courage beyond the fear. Being proactive is the method to becoming intentional. You must contemplate your options and then take action to accomplish the objective.

But what if you don't know what your options are? Therein lies the most basic problem of problems: You don't know what you don't know. You must seek wisdom from someone who has the answers to your questions.

I love when I see the tide of change come in, that moment when the teacher becomes student, and I begin to be schooled by my clients. That's the moment when I know they will be fine. I love to hear the passion that bubbles up in session where my clients get up and pace in my office. They passionately formulate in their minds the pathways they are creating and begin to speak their truth. Their words, their actions, and their energy dramatically changed from one extreme (weak) to the other (strength), and they are internally motivated to live the life they desire, not the one that was handed them.

The process of change has begun, and they are now picking up steam and driving it home.

Once such moment happened recently. Sometime ago, I met Reggie (not his real name; all names have been changed to protect the individual's identity). He came to me heartbroken and suicidal. A series of events left him questioning his value as a man, husband, and father. When he spoke, he was defeated, deflated, and without hope. Change was not easy for him, but he remained willing to learn. Week after week, the evidence of his perceptions were reinforced and further devalued his self-image. Ongoing struggles to change others in his life continued to barricade him from real change. Then something happened that changed everything. He quit trying to change his environment and started to change himself. Through a series of small, focused baby steps, Reggie began to explore other possibilities, change habits, and the changed results encouraged him. The more he accomplished, the more he desired. The more he desired, the more effort he made. The more effort he made, the more change he saw. The momentum of change began to carry him to the point where he was so passionate about his new life that he revealed his new truth to me.

"When we focus on remaining positive, only doors to positivity will open to us. When we say we can't, we are only defeating ourselves. We need to make the best of each day and live it to the fullest. I'm going to be consumed with my present moment, right now. This is my future. If I can be happy here, then I'm living my best life now."

Success can be your servant or your master.

This book is intended to provide some basic life skills and concepts for creating a paradigm shift of thinking. In changing your thinking, you will begin to change your behaviors and your choices. Consequently, you'll have a better and more intentional outcome. It is impossible for one book to provide you all the answers you need to become the best version of yourself. I heard years ago that the average person never reads another book after they graduate high school. There is a proven correlation between wisdom and the reading of books. About 10 percent of college students graduate with a bachelor's degree, 3 percent go on to get a master's degree, and only 1 percent will pursue a doctorate degree or open a business. If you read *one* book a month on topics that you have little to no wisdom, at the end of one year you'd have read more books and gained more wisdom than 90 percent of the population. There's a reason the most educated make the most money as knowledge is the foundation of success. Ask for advice from people who are capable, not your friends or family members who can't even make their own good life choices. Additionally, not all friends or family members make bad choices either. Don't go to your broke friends asking financial advice, and don't go to your abuser to ask their advice how to leave. There is wisdom in the books of those who lived before us. Books encourage, enlighten, and provide us pathways to living an intentional life. I hope this book does as well.

> *Plans fail for lack of counsel, but with many advisers they succeed.* (Proverbs 15:22 NIV)

CHAPTER 2

Intentional Faith

*Faith is the substance of things hoped for,
the evidence of things not seen.*
—Hebrews 11:1 (NKJV)

What is faith? Faith is not a church, synagogue, or temple. It is not found in tangible things like crosses and crucifix, golden goblets or books. You may climb every mountain and walk through every valley, fly to the moon and beyond, but faith is not going to mystically appear so you can have it. You cannot acquire faith from your parents, your pastor, or your teachers. You don't inherit it as a family legacy, and you cannot purchase it. You may learn a form of faith, but if it is not supported by evidence of truth, you may have a misguided faith supported by lies. Faith is truth, and what you believe to be true is supported by evidence of that truth.

Everyone has faith of one type or another, and even when they say they don't believe in God, they have faith that he must exist in order for them to reject him. They don't want the consequences for their choices, so they reject the ultimate judge who can condemn them. Faith is not God but how you believe there is a God. Faith is knowing, and that knowing gives you confidence in how to live. You accept the consequences for poor choices because you know the benefit of it. When you believe in God, you can have hope. Without God, life has no meaning, no joy, and everything is temporary. When you have no faith or have lost it, you also lose confidence because you question what you believe to be true. Faith in God makes all things possible as faith has nothing to do with our own limited abilities but having confidence in God's unlimited abilities. Faith is a living concept that must be nourished, fed, and encouraged to grow. When your faith increases, your confidence increases as well as what you believe is reinforced by the truth. When you know what you believe is true, and you live in that truth, that is when you are living an intentional faith.

How you live your life reveals your faith.

I have witnessed how change manifests drastically different in someone who has faith versus someone without faith. The person who feels they are not alone in their struggle and who expects divine intervention does not experience as much stress, anxiety, or depression as someone who goes through very similar challenges without faith. Just knowing they are not alone in the battle helps them press through the challenges before them because they have faith that extends beyond themselves.

The person who lacks faith finds themself up against a challenge they don't have confidence in themselves to solve, so they feel stuck and give up. They can't see a way around the struggle, and so the struggle is insurmountable, impossible, and impractical to resolve. The person of faith learns to *give* those challenges to God, and in time, they wait for the solutions to appear. Do they always? No, but they don't have to collapse under the weight of not knowing the answers because they trust the answers will be revealed. They find peace in knowing they don't need to have all the answers or power within themselves. They know God's power is greater than their own. All they need is patience to wait, to believe, and have faith.

Action

I love a messy eater. I love how people will dive into a meal at Christmas or Thanksgiving with reckless abandonment. They act as if they haven't eaten for weeks, and that this meal is the best they've ever had. Compliments are given to the cook, and the cook receives those compliments gladly. In some cultures, the cook will not eat until their guest has finished their meal followed by a resounding belch. The cook may now enjoy their own meal knowing the food was enjoyed by their guest.

I am a messy eater when it comes to consuming the Word of God. My Bible is beaten, torn, and marked from cover to cover from yellow highlighters and underlined scripture. When I was a new Christian, I saw a woman in her nineties open her battered Bible, and on every page she flipped through, every word was marked, highlighted, or underlined. She told me she had read the Bible front to back so many times that the words were becoming difficult to read, and she would be forced to purchase a new Bible. I realized that keeping my pristine Bible nicely protected and clean was not the best way to learn. I determined then to consume the words, meditate on their meanings, and intentionally sought to improve my understanding. Over the years, I have purchased other Bibles, study Bibles, various translations, and some that have specific people in mind like the one Bible I have for military personnel. I have Bibles of different sizes and some that even have elaborate pictures. My family Bible weighs about twenty-five pounds and is five inches thick. It is filled with art that covers full pages and has our family history that covers eight generations. This Bible I do not mark up. I cherish the thought that one day, I will pass it on to my grandchildren's children.

I wish everyone was forced to purchase a new Bible because of their messy faith. I fear if we are not getting messy enough in our faith, our faith may fall away never to be recovered. Faith is not just a feeling but a commitment. It is not a title but is a personal choice. Faith is developed through a relationship with God. Like all relationships, you must share time with God, letting him know your fears, hurts, and needs as well as the desires of your heart. God is not a genie waiting to award you three wishes. He knows you, and he has a desire for you to know him. He wants you to follow him willingly. This is why you should never take your faith for granted. You never fall into faith, and you should never follow God blindly.

Sometimes, faith can feel like you're flying blind. You can't see where you're going or what is ahead of you. All you know is where you've been. You can easily focus on your past mistakes because you know them so intimately. Getting stuck in feelings of regret can give you a sense of being grounded, but grounded won't get you anywhere. You were born to fly, but flying blind is scary, and fear holds you back. This is where having a faith that is supported by truth can change everything. Faith is a choice, and because it is a choice, you can approach your faith intentionally.

Faith exists beyond the pages of the Bible. Hebrews 11 frames faith in terms of historical context. Each paragraph brings to memory the life of a biblical character who acted in faith. When we know the past, we can plan confidently for the future.

Faith has its foundations rooted in everything you know and believe. It is the air, water, and earth. It is the family that surrounds you and the one that abandoned you. It is your past, present, and your future. Faith is everywhere and nowhere all at the same time. Faith exists even if you don't want it. We live and walk in faith as it is the core of humanity. Everyone has faith, even when you say you don't; the fact that you believe you don't is your faith.

Every day at my practice as a therapist, I see faith in action. People who have experienced all types of traumas are seeking ways to relieve their mental wounds and broken hearts. They are taking a leap of faith as they put their trust in a complete stranger who they hope will have the advice they need. I see the development of faith as having four action steps: fear, vulnerability, courage, and conviction.

Fear

We all are afraid of something. Fear is one of the first emotions we experience upon entering the world at birth when we left our mother's womb—a place of comfort, warmth, and security. Unfortunately, we will spend the rest of our lives trying to find comfort, warmth, and security. Every step we take, we risk falling. Every breath we take may be our last. Every high is followed by lows, and with each defeat, we fear we may never recover. It is easy to feel fear.

All we have to do is consider the possibilities for something to go wrong. We can live in fear as we try to adjust to our environment and control our thoughts that lead to fear. Fear begins in our minds, travels to our bodies, and is felt by everyone around us. There is a saying that people can "smell" fear in someone who is afraid. The more intense we feel fear, the more intense our reaction to it. We may begin by avoiding things that make us fearful, like heights, elevators, planes, spiders, and snakes. We may feel a panic attack when we fear we cannot avoid or escape the situation. We may run, hide, or collapse to the floor. Fear can also motivate us. It can urge us into battle where fear of death can push us to succeed. Winston Churchill said, "Fear is a reaction. Courage is a decision." I believe before you can be courageous, you must first be willing to be vulnerable, and that's where fear lives.

Vulnerability

When I entered a career in law enforcement, I realized that I was making a conscientious decision that I might possibly die in service to another. But the decision to sacrifice my life was not the same as putting myself out there to prove it. I may say "I'll take a bullet," but if I never leave the station, am I truly vulnerable? We cannot be vulnerable without taking a risk. I had to be willing to leave safety and put myself in harm's way. I had to be willing to risk my life in order to save another. Every day of my career, I had to realize I was sacrificing myself and all my tomorrows to save the life of someone today. Everyone who serves others is taking a risk, and risk comes in many ways. We can risk our security financially, relationally, and emotionally. We can have risks that we alone may consider, but often, we must consider how our decisions affect others. I was a single mom, and if I lost my life in service, my daughter would have no parent to love and care for her. We must consider the risk before we can decide to be vulnerable. If the risk is worth the reward, we then make the decision that leads to us to courage.

Courage

Recently, I was listening to the radio and callers were asking, "How can I learn to be courageous?" The host gave his opinion rather sheepishly, "I think you either have it or you don't." I immediately wanted to call and say, "That's not true." Everyone can have courage. Everyone has experienced it to some degree, but few master it. Courage does not happen accidentally. Courage must be intentional.

Courage is faith under fire. It happens when you are faced with a difficult, challenging, even impossible decision, and you do the right, necessary, or forced action anyway. It's that moment in the last heartbeat before stepping out of the airplane where you give your life over to faith. You hold dear to what you know about the parachute, and you believe it will open even when you have no certainty that it will. When you reach the end of knowledge, faith is all you have. When people don't have faith, it's hard to be courageous. For people who have faith, the stronger their faith is, the more courageous they can be. Repeated confidence that you are doing what is right and just leads us to conviction.

Conviction

A conviction is not the same as a commitment as commitments are broken all the time. Our convictions are rooted in what we believe to be true. Once we know truth, we must seek, speak, and live the truth. Our convictions may be based in what our parents told us, what we learned in school, and what society shows us in social media. I recall how political hacks of the 1960s treated our military personnel who had gone to fight a war the politicians started. Young men and women with a conviction to serve and protect were only following orders. Today, politicians continue to start wars, far and near, because there is great financial profit to be made. When something is broken, we must fix it. One party builds up businesses; the other tears them down and burns them to the ground. One builds an economy that encourages independence; the other tells you dependence on government is the only way to succeed. One says the power should be in the hands of the people; the other says the people can't be trusted. These two contradictions in terms cannot coexist, and eventually, one will give way to the other. Where greed and personal gain is the primary goal of our politicians, the people lose. Like sheep following our leaders to the edge of a cliff, we obey them and jump. As we fall to our destruction, we hope what we see is not really happening because the truth is too much to comprehend and, therefore, unbelievable.

Some people become so convicted in believing a lie because it's easier than considering the truth. They would have to be open to listening to another possibility that may prove them wrong, and this could mean they would have to change their entire belief system. Consider the race wars that always seem to get ignited by politicians and promoted by special interest groups who have no desire to change anything but love to be on stage yelling, waving flags, and taking government payoffs. Who is benefitting from the chaos, destruction, and death? The same politicians who receive money to fix the problems they create. This pattern is repeated all through history, which is why they want to destroy history. By eliminating anything to compare their behaviors with, we are more likely to naively follow their demands. When we can kill off those who have memories of the past, the new version of history (lies) will replace the truth of the past, and history will repeat because that is their goal. What worked before will work again. They just don't want you to see what's coming. They need you to believe and commit to the lie, which requires you to compromise what you know to be true.

This is where faith is the measurement for truth, not opinion. Opinion can be compromised, and we can change our minds in a moment. I measure everything I know—my beliefs, my knowledge, and understanding—against the belief and knowledge others present to me, and I look to the Bible as the standard for truth. When the truth contradicts what I know, I follow my faith. When it contradicts the opinion of others, I consider the truth and follow what my faith tells me to do. When the standard of truth is consistent, it's easy to follow. Bottom line: I'd rather live with faith than die without it. This is my conviction and one I won't compromise.

Compromise

We all seek safety from the things we fear and are willing to compromise everything, including our faith, in order to feel secure. Compromise kills faith. It happens slowly through a series of choices that compromises our beliefs. It is a step in the wrong direction, that first drink, that first high, that first temptation that we allow ourselves to explore. We know it is not good for us, but we do it anyway. There are many reasons we compromise our faith. We may see a better way of believing that leads to a sense of enlightenment, enrichment, or entitlement. We alter our beliefs to avoid feelings of guilt and shame. We don't consider the consequences beforehand and may benefit from the lies we tell ourselves for many years to come. Eventually, the consequences find us. The consequences of our compromise will hit us full force when we realize we are spiraling out of control and full of regret. How do we change this from happening? We must seek the truth, not what is popular. When you see that all roads lead to the same destination, question where they are taking you. Open your eyes and your mind and do as the Bible instructs us: test all things, hold onto the good, and reject the evil (1 Thessalonians 5:20–22). Know what you believe, fear nothing, be willing to be vulnerable, live courageously, and stand on your convictions that are rooted in truth.

What you put your faith in matters. Faith is not the same as hope, yet you can't have hope without faith. Hope gives you confidence that something is possible. Faith is knowing that nothing is impossible. Faith is where miracles happen. Faith goes beyond confidence in self, beyond hoping in others, beyond all understanding, wisdom, or knowledge. Usually, people find their faith in that moment when they have exhausted all their resources, used all their skills, applied all their knowledge, failed, and have lost all hope. It is at this point they drop to their knees and ask God for help. Intentional faith works backward from this. Start by asking God to help you as you enter the difficulty. Believe God is there beside you as you walk into the flames, enter a difficult conversation or step out of the plane. Faith means letting go of the need to control the outcome. *Intentional faith* is believing the outcome, whatever it is, will be the outcome that's meant to happen. Good or bad, fair or unjust, all decisions made in faith are hard. It's not courage that helps you step out of the plane. Courage is the reward you receive once you safely land on the ground and look back at how much courage it took to step out in faith. Once you have evidence rooted in historical context, you can repeat the actions with confidence of a positive outcome. The evidence comes from knowing, and knowing comes from the evidence of what was first true, is true today, and remains to be true for all time.

> I will sing of the Lord's great love forever; with my mouth I will make your faithfulness known through all generations. (Psalm 89:1 NIV)

CHAPTER 3

Intentional Mindset

"For my thoughts are not your thoughts, neither
are your ways my ways," declares the Lord.
—Isaiah 55:8 (NIV)

There are different types of mindsets. They can be rigid, unbending, and resistant to change, or they can be pliable, flexible, and eager to change. They can be spontaneous or calculating. They can be free flowing or stagnant. They can be open to new ideas, or they can be closed. So how can we have an intentional mindset? First, you must learn which mindset you have. From there, the rest is easy. Sort of.

Ancient philosophers talked about how the mind is rooted in the soul in one of three parts that makes us uniquely human: *body*, *mind (soul)*, and *spirit*.

The *body* is everything physical, sexual, and is the neediest part of our existence. When we move through choices, it is our body that first must satisfy its needs. We must eat, drink, rest, and expel energy and excess waste. The body experiences life through touch, smell, taste, hearing, and seeing, but it is the mind that interprets those experiences and gives them meaning.

Our *mind* responds to the urges of our body by complying or denying them. We can restrict our eating or overeat. We can exercise or sit on the couch. We can use our body to accomplish great things, or we can give in to temptations that lead us toward destruction. The body is nothing without the direction of the mind. We see this when someone is in a comma, the body lays limp and unresponsive. Conversely, we can see how paralysis does not limit what the mind is capable of, but without the body to take care of the mind, it falters, sputters, and stops as in the case of Alzheimer's and dementia. Much of what the mind determines is influenced by our will, and that is found in the spirit.

The *spirit* is what God breathed into Adam that gave him life. It is the inherent part of our being that knows when something is right or wrong, good or bad, healthy or unhealthy. It is where happiness and joy, sorrow, and grief, and guilt and shame reside. Our mind may make the decisions, but it's the spirit that judges us.

When I think of how to explain these components in simple to understand terms, I use the analogy of a car. The body is the beautiful aspects of the car and what attracts our initial attention. The body goes beyond the shell and includes all the moving parts that require constant maintenance and attention as it shakes, rattles, and rolls along. The mind is the steering wheel that determines where the body will go. And the spirit is the gas that gives the car movement and momentum. Without consideration for spiritual things, we may do and think whatever we want, but we will have a poor sense of direction and may have very little momentum.

So how can we be mindful and intentional? I don't believe you can be intentional without being mindful, but you can be mindful and unintentional as determined by your choices that are either wise or weak-minded.

What does it mean to be weak-minded? It is when we give others power over our mind. We don't have the strength to control our thoughts, and when our thoughts run wild, they control our bodies, and that affects our emotions. Our mind will believe whatever we tell it. Whatever we think is our truth is our reality. Whatever we believe to be true, our body and our emotions will affirm to be true. If we believe someone has ill plans for us and has a desire to cause us harm, we will act defensively toward them. If we are afraid, it is because we think in terms that create fear. If we feel anxious, it's because we have thoughts that create worry. Over time, if we don't get these thoughts under control by challenging them with truth and evidence that is contrary to our personal beliefs, we can develop mental health problems, such as anxiety with panic attacks driven by fear, depression, and even have suicidal thoughts. Our negative thoughts are directly linked to rewiring the brain to believe lies, and our body responds by living in an elevated state of stress that can lead to all sorts of health problems.

Do you get easily overwhelmed? Do you wake anxiously as your mind makes a to-do list of chores that require your immediate attention? Do you rush through your day only to collapse on the couch in front of the TV? Do you feel exhausted, frustrated, and trapped in a pattern that you can't seem to break?

You're not alone.

Anxiety has become the acceptable norm in society today. Everyone is experiencing pressure to perform to higher and higher expectations being pressed upon them by others. Those in power are becoming more demanding, and those who have to comply are feeling more and more anxious. When my clients come to therapy, I can see the worry on their furrowed brows, the pent-up energy in their bouncing legs, and their confusion and pain in their hand-wringing. Their bodies are ready to explode, and they are keeping the lid on their lives pressed down as hard as they can. This is no way to live.

I teach my clients that it is good to perform and strive for excellence, but they must put as much energy into resting as they do in performing. I call this type of focused relaxation "performance rest." People who are performance driven (by external or internal reasons) need to find success in resting. Unfortunately, rest for these types of people is seen as a deterrent to success, a barrier to time, and is a consequence, not a reward for hard work. In order to change one's mindset to performance rest, it is necessary to see rest as something to pursue and not an annoyance to tolerate.

A friend of mine understands this concept well. He is a performer and knows that if he wants to be successful as a singer, he must *rest* his voice. It's good to recognize you need rest before your voice starts straining. Resting while playing musical instruments is good for you as well. As an athlete, we must rest in order to be at peak performance, and brainiacs need rest as well. When you do *performance rest*, you take breaks more often. Consequently, you will recover from the challenges of the day quicker. When we are tired, we can be irritable. Rest relieves the stress and can give us an attitude adjustment. Babies need naps, and sometimes moms do too. When you wake, you'll feel better, have a better outlook, and others will enjoy you more. You just might like yourself a little better too.

Teach

When I was in college, one of my favorite subjects was philosophy. Recently, I was reminded how philosophical constructs of the past still apply to current circumstances. Have you ever heard of the Allegory of the Cave by philosopher Plato? What is an allegory? It is a fictional story that has a purpose for teaching and not merely for entertainment. Plato's Allegory of the Cave represents how a changed perspective and learning the truth can be painful but worth the journey.

Plato speaks about an underground cave where people have been confined since early childhood. They are chained and are only able to the see shadows on the wall before them. Behind them is a raised fire and a half wall. Puppet masters hide behind the wall and raise carved figures into the firelight that projects a shadow of the figure onto the wall before the prisoners. They hear noises and speaking from behind them, but the shadows are all they see. They are left to their imaginations and contemplations among themselves as to the meaning and truth of what is before them. The puppet masters determine the story and, consequently, the truth of the shadows.

Plato says that one of the prisoners finds himself released and brought to see the fire, the wall, and the puppet masters. His eyes hurt from the light, and his mind reels as he learns a new truth. His captors take him to the mouth of the cave where he is exposed to direct sunlight and the world aboveground. This is a very painful experience, both for his eyes and his mind. Everything he believed is now shattered as his perspective is shown to have been totally wrong. He is exposed to reality, and this new understanding (enlightenment) cannot be undone.

He returns to the cave with a desire to share his experience with the others. When he steps out of the light and into the depth of the cave, his eyes have trouble adjusting, and he stands momentarily blinded. He attempts to share what he has seen above, but the prisoners reject his perspective and question his sanity. They don't want to leave the safety of the cave and everything they know and so remain in the dark.

Plato challenges his students to consider how difficult it is to gain knowledge of the truth, and sometimes we must be pulled from our comfort to learn what is real. He also shows that the enlightened prisoner has an obligation to return to the uneducated people and bring them into the light. We are living a real-life allegory between darkness and light, what is real and what is true, and many are watching the shadows placed before them by puppet masters. Others have chosen to break free of the chains and step into the light.

When I was researching Plato's original translation of the allegory, I was appalled that one site for teachers made the allegory about how teachers must "drag" their students to what the teacher determines to be true. That sounds more like the puppet masters' approach to learning and not Plato's. Yes, it can be painful when you learn what you thought to be true is a lie, and sometimes the teacher must be patient with the student's resistance to change, but when exposed to the truth and what is real, it can bring you to a place where you can see more clearly. Once you know the truth, you have an obligation to share that truth with others so they also may be set free.

What you choose to focus on will be your focus in everything. When you focus on porn, you will see everyone through the lens of sex. When you focus on hate, everything will have no value. When you focus on love, grace, God, and his blessings, giving thanks in all things, you will receive all of God's grace, love, and strength.

Memories

Bad moments often can become some of our best memories. Think back at some of the most humorous moments you've had with friends and family. When I was in law enforcement, we used to meet after work for a weekly *debriefing*. We would recall moments of the past week when we were the most scared. We would all laugh at stories of overcoming our fears, and they would ensure us that bravery would arise again for the next difficult challenge. We were told we were courageous, and so we believed it. This positively reinforced our belief in ourselves as everyone desired to be courageous, even when we didn't feel we could.

Working in law enforcement taught me to believe in myself. When I was injured in the academy and forced to leave, I was devastated. I had dreamed of being a cop since I was eleven years old. For weeks following the incident, I was crushed. Then something happened to me, I became determined to change my circumstances by changing me. I went from a weak mindset to one of strength and determination. For the next year, everything I did, everything I read, every moment of every day was intentional. One year later, I was running ten miles a day, doing one hundred push-ups, and two hundred sit-ups. I did burpees until my legs burned, and I pressed on for ten more. When I returned to the police academy, I was strong in both mind and body, and as a result, I exceeded all expectations.

Difficulty opens the door to opportunity.

When I have clients who feel life is pressing down on them from all sides, I ask them to focus on where the growth opportunities are. Most of the time, they have no idea what I'm talking about. They may tell me they are "overwhelmed," "tired," or "frustrated" with their life. They look at all the reasons to be miserable and have trouble finding any silver lining in the middle of a depressive torrential downpour. But with fresh eyes, anyone can find something to be thankful for. In today's world of ongoing problems, it's easy to worry about tomorrow. So day after day, we miss the blessings of our moments with family, friends, and loved ones. I recall learning about a father who was sitting in the middle of a battle singing with his little girl and using the booming of the artillery as if they were symbols of a drum. Paul the Apostle wrote some of the most encouraging words in the New Testament while he sat in a Roman prison awaiting his execution. His advice to us? Be thankful. Gratitude makes us focus on the blessings we have, even when we have every reason not to be thankful.

Look at every challenge as a way for God to send you blessings. When COVID-19 hit the world and the schools closed to in-person education and parents were being sent home from work because they also had been forced closed, suddenly, families were together. If they had focused on the blessing of the moment, they would have survived the epidemic stronger as a family. Unfortunately, many families suffered from the changes instead of taking advantage of them.

Many years ago, a good friend of mine gave me this advice when, due to an injury, I was forced into an early retirement. I was complaining about the loss of income and the uncertainty of my future when she said, "Aren't you always complaining that you never have time with your daughter because all you do is work? And when you have time, you complain you never have money?" I agreed, and she said, "Right now, you have both time and money, and you're still complaining?"

I took a moment to consider this new truth and made the decision to enjoy the blessings I had been given. That next year was one of the most memorable and enjoyable years of my life because I made a decision to be both mindful and intentional. If you only look at the challenge and the difficulty, even long after the problem has been resolved, you will never see the blessings you missed.

There are many examples in the Bible how God wants us to be intentionally mindful, how we should think, behave, and set boundaries with others. One such story is of Adam and Eve in the garden of Eden. God created the tree of knowledge of good and evil (Genesis 2:9) and warned Adam that on the day he eats from it, he shall die (Genesis 2:17). Notice this was before Eve even enters the story (Genesis 2:21). Eve got tricked by the serpent (Satan) and ate and then gave Adam a bite too. When they ate the fruit from the forbidden tree, they immediately felt guilt and shame because they knew they broke God's rule (Genesis 3:3), and sin entered Adam and Eve and everyone thereafter (Genesis 3:15). Even though we have free will, the Bible warns us that everything is permissible, but not everything is beneficial (1 Corinthians 10:23). Our decisions hurt not only our body and mind but also our spirit. When we live a life that is not mindful and intentional, it's like spending our days polishing a beautiful car that we never take out of the garage. Life is so much better when you take that beauty out on the road, propelled by the Spirit living in you. Many times in the therapeutic setting, I recommend to my clients they romanticize the life they want to design and how soon they wish to begin. Remember, New Year's resolutions don't have to wait for a date on the calendar.

> *Do not be anxious about anything, but in every situation, by prayer and petition, with thanksgiving, present your requests to God.* (Philippians 4:6 NIV)

CHAPTER 4

Intentional Character

Those who guard their lips preserve their lives, but those who speak rashly will come to ruin.
—Proverbs 13:3 (NIV)

The year 2020 brought on the coronavirus pandemic. The year 2021 revealed something more deadly than any variant we could perceive. What was revealed was our selfish nature, greed, and murderous hearts. We live in a world where bad behavior is rewarded and good behavior is ridiculed, shamed, and criticized. Convicted criminals found *guilty* in a court of law are randomly set free, and victims' cries for justice are ignored. When the offenders commit new crimes, even to the extent of murder, their new victims are held accountable, and the offender again suffers no consequences. At the time of this writing, prisons are closing, and convicted criminals are set free by the tens of thousands. Antifa and Black Lives Matter riots continue unabated, terrorizing and destroying entire communities. Meanwhile, our borders are left unprotected, and we are importing terrorists by the thousands. The constitutional laws that govern our land are being ignored or are being torn down like the statues of our past. In schools, our children are being indoctrinated with lies, and hate speech has become so common on television we are desensitized and numb to its effects. We are at war within our own families as we take sides to express our beliefs concerning what is true.

Critical thinking has evaded even the most scholarly who have given away their individuality for the benefits of belonging. Many willingly accept the terms and conditions put upon them by others as a condition for receiving free benefits. Others fight against tyranny and the loss of freedoms while they struggle to maintain their individuality and self-control. Hate has replaced love, fear snuffs out courage, and paralysis has replaced action. We have become a nation who is sleepwalking, and if we don't wake up soon, we may find there is no waking from this nightmare.

Society as a whole has been sold a package of lies. We have been told that if we fall in line with the lies and manipulations of others, we will be taken care of. Yet the ones who are telling us what character should be are not even following their own guidelines. People who have no character do not have the right to tell others what their character should look like, yet we accept their definitions without challenge. When we try to live up to their unrealistic and ever-changing guidelines, we become anxious as our attempts to comply are never enough. We become anxious and depressed while the ones in charge continue to get richer and more powerful, all the while enjoying their freedoms and libations. They feast on food and drink while the masses stand in lines fighting for limited resources, food, toilet paper, and water. They vote for pay increases for themselves while putting middle- and low-class Americans out of work. They raise taxes to pay for favors abroad and reduce opportunities for earning an income here. In other words, the rich get richer, and the poor remain poor. The middle class falls further away from the middle as they find themselves part of the unemployed, broke, and homeless. So how can we change all this doom and gloom to resemble a life worth living? It starts with *character*.

Why is character so important, and why should we be intentional with it? Because you won't fight for something unless it's something you believe in. If you don't know who you are, how can you fight for you? For decades, good people have been told what they believe is wrong and your beliefs are intolerant and judgmental. The words of Jesus have been taken out of context and used as a weapon against those who desire to be good. So in order to be seen as good, people began to compromise what they knew to be true and became more tolerant of untruths. Once individual beliefs and convictions were removed, and people became more tolerant of the lies, tolerance was no longer the desired standard, and acceptance became the new measurement for compromise. When acceptance became the standard, and people again compromised their beliefs, inclusion became the new standard. When inclusion tore away the last shreds of compromise, compliance became the new standard, and the nation woke up to having no rights, no power, and no idea how to fight their way out of the box they allowed themselves to be put in. It all started with compromise, and what we compromised was the truth.

Truth

Recently, I heard someone speaking about their husband's character, "He's not tactful, but he is truthful." Even though she said the delivery of the truth can sometimes be painful to hear, she appreciates that he is always honest with her. The world we live in makes one appreciate honesty and grieve the lack of it. Everywhere, dishonesty rules the day, and the resulting confusion leaves us feeling lost and alone.

Lies destroy us in the workspace, the neighborhood, and in the home. Fear of the unknown has created a generation who fear walking out their front door. We have become prisoners of our own making, and living has been replaced by merely surviving. But what are we truly afraid of? Pain? Suffering? Death? When we are afraid of pain, we will avoid risk. When we are afraid of suffering, we become physically and mentally weak. When we are afraid of death, we become unable to live. All this can be reversed, but it takes a strong mind, body, and spirit. We must challenge the lies that we have heard and replace them with the truth. We must look for people we can trust and avoid those who are not trustworthy. Remember, a partial truth is still a lie, and when you accept the partial truth, you also accept the lie.

Here are a couple things to be aware of that will let you know if the person is being dishonest with you. I call it the Flip, Flop, Flam:

- *Flip.* When you catch them in a lie, do they redirect the attention to your misdeeds, flaws, or lies?
- *Flop.* Do they make excuses for their lies and accuse you of being unloving, uncaring, or insensitive?
- *Flam.* Do they convince, attack, or demand you must trust them even when they are caught repeatedly telling lies?

When people constantly do the flip-flop-flam approach to answering your questions and concerns, they are avoiding the truth and are not worthy of your trust. When they refuse to acknowledge their lies, they also refuse to take responsibility for them. People avoid change by refusing to acknowledge there is a need for change. When their goal is to manipulate and control you, they will never change. Change for them means relinquishing control back to you, and this is unacceptable for them. When you see the lies and truth of the matter, you are left with two options: stay the same or change yourself. Start living your truth even when they won't. Speak the truth even if they refuse to hear it. Set expectations, and if they are not met, you need to be ready to enforce consequences, even if that means leaving. You can also choose to do nothing and make the choice to live a lie that you know is clearly not true. This option will result in you living in pain and suffering until you die. But heck, it's the devil you know, and it's easier than the unknown. Or is it? When you know the truth and willingly live the lie, you will beat yourself down, your self-esteem with suffer, and the pain you feel will be self-inflicted. The truth will always find a way to reveal itself, and you know it.

Take baby steps that lead to clear thinking and understanding. When you know the truth and acknowledge the truth, you won't need anyone else to agree with it. You just know it's true, and you have the evidence to support it. Just acknowledging the truth begins the process of change. You will begin to see other areas where lies prevail. You are now more aware of the truth, and that leads to more truth and more understanding, and then more truth is revealed. One day, when you can see all the areas where you have been living with lies, you'll want to live the truth. On that day, you'll discover that you have the courage to walk out the door.

- Love is freely given, but don't waste your love on anyone who is not worthy of your love. "Do not give dogs what is sacred; do not throw your pearls to pigs. If you do, they trample them under their feet, and turn and tear you to pieces" (Matthew 7:6).
- Don't give your finances to anyone who you expect won't repay the loan; unless you give it freely and without expectation. "The rich rule over the poor, and the borrower is slave to the lender" (Proverbs 22:7).
- Don't share your emotional hurts and pains with someone who will use that information against you. "Bitterly she weeps at night, tears are on her cheeks. Among all her lovers there is no one to comfort her. All her friends have betrayed her; they have become her enemies" (Lamentations 1:2).
- Don't trust anyone who is not trustworthy. "Trust in the Lord with all your heart and lean not on your own understanding" (Proverbs 3:5).

Trust is a precious gift that should be shared with very few. Those few will have proven to be trustworthy over time with consistent words and actions that match. If they say they will, they do. If they say yes, they mean it. If they are honest, even to the point of hurting your feelings, they are a trustworthy friend. You may only have one of two of these types of friends in a lifetime. When you realize there are more people to doubt than those you can believe, intentionally seek out honest people; you'll be more likely to succeed in finding someone worthy of your trust.

Men

All across America, men have forgotten who they are and have lost their purpose in life. They were once men made of iron, but the metal has collapsed under the weight of fear and loss.

I was working in my office when a marine came in and sat in a chair across from me. He was built like the action figure Iron Man, only he wore no suit of armor. His muscles bulged under his shirt and his six-foot-five-inch stature was imposing. He looked into my eyes, and I saw they were filled with fear. He cautiously spoke about his world collapsing around him where nightmares stole his sleep and his days were consumed by anger. He was a man who had been to Afghanistan and Iraq several times and had seen things too horrific to share. The weight of those memories were tearing him apart, but it was the fear of losing himself as he approached the end of his twenty years in service that brought him to his knees. He was terrified of the uncertainty of his future and the possibility of not being able to care for his wife and six children.

Another gentleman came to me for help with his relationship which had begun to crumble following his girlfriend's discovery of his having an affair with a woman he cared nothing about. He shared that he had met his current girlfriend while married to his ex-wife who left him and took the kids when she learned of the affair. He lost his wife, his children, and his home, and here he was doing it again. On the verge of losing his military career, the thought of losing his girlfriend meant he was one step away from becoming homeless.

A third man walked through my door and collapsed on the floor. He broke down sobbing and shared his pain about the recent death of his father and the loss of his wife and child to a recent divorce. The grief was heavy on him, and I listened while my heart ached for his situation. Over the next few months, I offered compassion and care, but the fear in his eyes as he stumbled over challenge after challenge was hard to watch. This was a man lost in regret over the past he could not change.

Stories like these are common occurrences today. What do these men have in common? They are all suffering from loss, fear, and a lack of personal identity. All three of these men were once strong, confident, and service oriented, willing to die for the life of another. They knew without a doubt who they were. They had a purpose bigger than themselves and they took pride in their work. Then something changed, and they lost their way. They lost their confidence, passion, and purpose.

The collapsing of a soul is never easy to watch, and I've recently had to watch too many souls break under the weight of fear. I've also seen these men rediscover who they are and find a new life's purpose. When you know who you are, have confidence in yourself, and move toward fulfilling your purpose, you can live your life and not just survive it.

Berry Boyce, founder of *Mindful* magazine, wrote about the effects of the 2020 pandemic and how we are entering into a new era, "The tyranny of clock and calendar have been removed, which could be a relief, but the resulting anarchy is unsettling, and the future is a fog of question marks" (Fall 2020, p.72). Many would agree with this statement. When everyone's routines were shut down, chaos filled in the gap, and chaos was everywhere. The ones who benefited from the chaos resisted against the return to what was normal so that new rules and norms could be established. This does not mean the replacement laws were better or even benefitted the masses, but they were shoved down society's throat, and we are left beaten and bruised by it.

One of the most disturbing effects of these changes is the inability to find truth and the increased move away from anything that resembles truth. Truth is built on a foundation of fact supported by evidence. Truth is absolute and never confusing. It may not be what you want to hear, but it will remain the truth. Instead, we are facing a time where truth is not absolute; it is confusing, and the evidence proves it to be fiction, yet we are forced to believe it as truth. This has created divisive perspectives where compromise is impossible. Opinion has replaced evidence, passion has replaced compassion, and violence has replaced debate. Two polar paradigms have been pushed further and further away from center in order to support one perspective rooted in hate. Many are not interested in facts or truth as these concepts are now secondary to feelings.

Unfortunately, feelings are not facts, and you can't be both emotional and logical at the same time. Feelings don't discern reality. Feelings are emotions that begin in our belief system. Feelings support our concepts and *opinions* of truth, not truth itself. This is why it's hard to argue with someone who truly believes the lie is true. They will fight to the death to defend the lie. When they believe they have no value or others have no value, they can justify the destruction of self (suicide) or others (homicide). Only by seeking and finding the truth and acknowledging it as the truth can one standard of truth be established.

Women

Have you noticed how much we are giving away of ourselves to technology? *Spell-check* means we don't have to *know* how to spell, and calculators on our phones means we don't have to *know* how to add, subtract, or divide. We can "search" any topic we want to explore and believe without question whatever we are told. We search for more, know less, and as long as no one challenges our beliefs, we can live in ignorant bliss.

We've stopped thinking for ourselves and are acting more like sheep being led to slaughter than intelligent individual thinkers. How can we be so smart and have so many negative consequences in our life? Why are our partners so screwed up (in our opinion), our children so disconnected (even while we don't speak to them or make any attempt to connect), and our parents be so judgmental (even while we stand in judgment of them)?

There is nothing new under the sun. Every form of lie, cheat, and deceit has been tried before and much of it recorded in historical documentation. Our problem is we don't know what to look for in a person that makes them good, and yet naively, we believe everyone has good intentions. In reality, most people have evil intentions. Some have desires to take from you everything you own and don't give a hoot or a holler about you or your feelings. Ouch! Yes, the truth hurts sometimes, but it's still the truth. Women are allowing themselves to be hurt and harmed because they have believed that to be strong means to give your strength over to the power of another. I tell you the truth, we bought into the lies that allow others to control us, and it's time to stop believing them.

Trustworthy

One of the things I love about working with new therapists is their desire to better understand people and what makes some more prone to emotional dysregulation when others appear to be more balanced and healthier. A lot of this has to do with adaptability and strength of character. The bottom line is you can't feel something you don't feel, you can't believe something you don't believe, and you can't fake character because someone is always watching, even if the only one watching is you. Character is the foundational truth you stand upon. It can have cracks, chips, and flaws, but ultimately, it is always the measure by which you value yourself and how others will value you.

Scripture is awesome when you can appreciate that the Bible is God's collection of love letters to you. It has stories of men and women who failed, and yet God called them "lovely," "the rock," "righteous," and "a man after God's own heart." It's filled with advice as one of God's many names is "mighty counselor." The Bible contains wisdom in the books of Psalms and Proverbs where lessons are handed down through generations. It has teachable moments that include math (the building of the ark), astrology (heaven and earth), biology (man and woman), behavior analysis (temptation), and reasoning (how we think). It teaches us that our beliefs are first and foremost what sets the course of our lives. And it tells us we can learn and grow from our mistakes to become saints. The ultimate gift is that it gives us concrete examples of character like integrity, honesty, strong moral fiber, and care and concern for others. It also teaches us to have self-control, humility, and to do the right thing.

The Bible sets a standard for living rooted in historical truth. The Bible shows us how to avoid things that can harm us, like people with evil intentions who speak lies that deceive us. The Bible tells us to look at the character of someone before you trust them, to use discernment in making choices who to trust, and sets boundaries when trust is broken. A person of good character will have good intentions supported by good behaviors. A person with selfish intentions only thinks how they can benefit from the vulnerability of others. They also will be discovered by their inconsistent words and actions and never should be trusted.

When I help clients understand why they are conflicted in relationships with individuals who are displaying poor character traits (lies, affairs, addictions, abuse, etc.), I show them three measures for establishing trust and setting healthy boundaries:

1. *Trustworthy.* A person who is trustworthy is a person who's character you can predict because they are consistently trustworthy. They are people who have never stolen, lied, or abused you. They have words that encourage you, and they are supportive of you. They are trusted confidants who you can turn to for advice and who you can trust to tell you a perspective that would benefit you. They would come help you in the middle of the night, repay all loans, and they would never intentionally harm you. Most people will only have one or two of these types of lifelong friendships.

2. *Limited trust.* This person might be someone you work with, a family member, a new relationship, or a person you haven't seen in a long time. You might tell them limited information while you are measuring up their character. If they spread rumors, borrow without repaying, or you hear them blaming others for their problems (rumors), you might want to set some healthy boundaries on how much money you give them, don't lend them your car, and avoid sharing personal information that you don't want the world to know. They may be people who give you attention, but the focus is on themselves. They may not be terrible to hang out with, but usually their choices are not the best. They may bring chaos to the relationship, but they laugh a lot and are fun to be around. They don't mean to be irre-

sponsible, insensitive, or dramatic; they just are. Most of the people you meet will fall into this category.

3. *Not trustworthy*. Avoid this person at all costs. This person has displayed abuse in the past and caused you harm or harmed another. If they did cause harm, and it was intentional, defended, or they deflected responsibility and justified the abuse, assuredly, they will do it again and again. If you are not looking out for this type of person, or if you trust strangers too freely, you will attract this type of person as they are opportunistic and actively seek to take advantage of others. A growing portion of the population has begun to believe this type of behavior is acceptable. Profiting from the vulnerability of the weak makes this behavior more appealing. Blaming the weak for being weak justifies their criminal and abusive behaviors. They seek out others of like mind to support and defend their evil intentions. They have no conscience and will physically, emotionally, or financially steal your last breath. I'll say it again; avoid this person at all costs.

When you assess a person's character, you are assessing if they are trustworthy or not. This measurement should be applied to all people including your partner, relatives, friendships, employers, celebrities, and politicians. When words don't match behaviors, you are looking at someone with poor character and someone you shouldn't trust. People who have strength of character are committed, honest, and loving and will stand by the truth all the days of their life.

Anxiety

We are all in crisis, and it's time to wake up to reality. Children who have been intentionally abandoned, ignored, and forgotten are having daily panic attacks and suicidal thoughts. They are living in fear of the unknown and are either running away, fighting for their lives, or are paralyzed, obsessing over a multitude of problems, looking for solutions.

Parents are slowly waking up to the truth. They are facing the harsh reality of learning they have limited parental rights and are feeling fearful for their children's futures. Those who have the money to move away from their circumstances are running away, looking for a place that offers them a sense of safety. Many others have lost heart as they obediently acquiesce to the unrealistic demands of others. Many are praying for God to remove them from suffering as they impatiently await the rapture and fear they may not be taken. Others take comfort knowing they will be fine no matter what because they have hope in God's promise of salvation, and they hold on to a weak faith built on doubt. What is everyone afraid of? What makes us fearful? It seems like everything has gone crazy, and peace is nowhere to be found.

This is what anxiety does to us. Anxiety is driven by fear. Left out of control, fearful thoughts can increase as negative thoughts create more and more fearful thoughts. When you find your mind spiraling out of control, you can look to what fear is driving the insanity. Often, miscommunication or a lack of knowledge and understanding can be the beginning of creating a fearful thought. It's the "what ifs" that drive us crazy. Our imagination takes us on a journey right over a cliff. Our emotions support the fearful thoughts by driving us to do something, anything, to escape the anxious fears in our minds. By gaining understanding, seeking the truth in all situations, and by watching for evidence that supports that truth, then further increasing understanding and repeating the pattern, we can find truth. This truth will then stop our anxious fearful thoughts. It's the lies we believe that keep us trapped in our loop of fear.

Nature

I love nature because it's simple, honest, and true. What you see is what you get. There is no hidden agenda, no complaining, it asks nothing of me, and it gives joy to me always. Nature changes and is always fresh and new. It is consistent, and I can tell the time of the day by the rising of the sun and know the time of the month by the fullness of the moon. The temperatures give warning of the changing seasons, and each year, the seasons repeat.

I wish people could be more like nature and learn to adapt to become more simple, honest, and true.

Sometimes people would rather adapt to the lies they are told, and they tell themselves rather than face the truth. One client shared that she is learning from her mistakes so she won't repeat them. She said a mentor once told her the truth about her future is being created from the decisions she makes today. She said she took it to heart when he said, "I've given you a buffet of knowledge, and if you leave hungry, it's on you."

When lies tell you to pull back, and it feels right, the truth is you need to ignore your feelings and push forward. Otherwise, you are faced with no choice than to believe the lies and continue to suffer. So many times in therapy, I must show people that what they are suffering are consequences from their own choice to believe the lies instead of challenging the lies with evidence of the truth.

> *Sometimes people don't want to hear the truth*
> *because they don't want their illusions destroyed.*
> (Friedrich Nietzsche)

Lies that we accept sometimes are rooted in hope in an illusion. It is a dream, a wish, and it is so clear in our mind that we try to manifest in others the things that will make that dream come true. But they don't. We don't want to let go of the dream because reality seems like a nightmare. We fear the unknown, so we stay in the true nightmare we try to adapt to and pretend. We post on social media photos of a dream, while knowing the truth is that we are far from living the dream.

Often, the lies we believe as adults began when we were children. That's why it is easy to believe. When you accept the lies your parents, teachers, and peers tell you, that you are unworthy, that you are a victim, that you cannot change your future, and you believe them, then you will subconsciously look for evidence to support those lies. You will attract people who also believe those same lies, and you will feel supported in that false belief. Once you are surrounded by like-minded people, it's hard to see yourself any other way. This is when I show them the truth and evidence to support it. I show them the evidence that what they have believed so long is really a lie. Through a process of constant challenging of the lie, it's amazing how quickly the truth becomes the catalyst for increasing hope that change is possible.

When you hear repeatedly that you are the problem and *you* must change, maybe it's a sign that you have been projecting what is your responsibility to change onto someone else. Start believing you have the power to change and take responsibility for it. That power will enable you to adapt to a new change that will let the consequences remain with the problem and the person who created it. If they have bad behaviors, don't try to change them. Change the way you respond to them. If they are abusive, leave. If you want them to change and they won't, you change. And if that means separating to find a place of safety for you and your children, make it happen. You are not a tree; you have legs to walk away from an unhealthy situation. Stop hoping and wishing your partner, friend, parent, sibling, or boss will change so you can be happy. Make a choice to be happy and find ways to make it happen.

It is wise to watch what is happing in your life. Wisdom comes from learning, and you learn by watching. Even Jesus said we are not to be sleeping but are to "watch" (Mark 13:37) and be awake. I recommend you read all of Mark, chapter 13, because Jesus talks about the signs of the end times, the trials and suffering that is to come, and how believers in faith are to conduct themselves. The final message of the chapter is that we are commanded to watch. But it's difficult to watch others who are in pain and suffering. We want to *do* something. We pace, get anxious, and feel disheartened, discouraged, and fearful. When we give in to the temptation to be afraid, we can lose our balance, become weak, and will not be ready when the time comes to take action. There is no strength in weakness. Courage comes after we are afraid, and we become committed to act. Be strong, courageous, and endure the difficulties so you are ready to respond.

Strong

The attack on men and what defines a male is a direct attack against masculinity, and any expression of male strength is now profane. Men feel criticized, silenced, and marginalized. Pornography has taught men to seek pleasure first. They have willingly consumed porn that has led them into bondage of sexual addiction. The truth that one woman and one man might meet all sexual, emotional, and relational needs has been replaced by the lies against monogamy.

Women have bought into the lies that they don't need a man. They can make their own money and can receive more government financial assistance by increasing the number of their children. When they seek love, they are only seeking short connections that don't last with multiple partners who take more than they give. When they wake up to the reality that all their choices have trapped them in repeated brokenness, responsibility that is overwhelming, and financial poverty, they lose their strength, their power, and their ability to control their outcome.

According to recent data, single moms represent over 70 percent of households, and nearly a third live in poverty. Families have been abandoned by men and women by choice. By accepting the lies of others, women learned that it's hard to make it on their own, struggling with both career and home, and the result of a single-parent home is the children are abandoned by both parents. At the end of the day, the children are raising themselves.

There is a war against the family that has been building for decades and has reached a climax. For decades, men have been absent from the home, and the women and children are left to fend for themselves. The welfare system has encouraged single moms to repeat patterns entrenched by previous generations and are discouraged to think differently as they pass down a worldview that keep them entrenched in a cycle of poverty. No one saw it coming because it's all they knew. No one told them it could be any different, so they didn't try anything different. After all, what you believe determines your actions, and those actions reinforce those beliefs, even if they are not true.

The solution to breaking the chains that bind us to hopelessness and discouraged limitations is to think differently, independently, and uniquely. Men who had no male role models at home need to step back into their families and start to protect them again. Men need to stop popping and walking and stop breaking hearts and homes. Men need to step into their strength of character and take action to protect the women and children. Women need to seek truth. They need to be open to possibilities, expand their understanding, and be willing to change. The men may be the protectors of the home, but the woman holds the key to teaching the next generation the truth. Change the narrative you've believed and seek not what is common but what is uncommon. Don't do what others tell you to do; do what you know to be right, true, and that which will lead you toward excellence. When men step back into the family and provide for them, when women grow in knowledge and truth, in the end, they will receive the respect they desire, a love that will not fail, and the hope of a better tomorrow. It all starts with character.

Excellence

In today's world, character doesn't seem to matter much. When we threw out any ability to judge another person according to one universal standard, character was thrown out as well. Good character is closely intertwined with morality, and when the definition of a moral person changed, bad character filled the void. Do you doubt what I say? How much consideration have you given to your own character and moral standards? Character traits are targets we should be striving toward. They are not intended to beat us down or make us feel inadequate. But if you are feeling bad because you are not living up to your own beliefs, your negative feelings could be that your internal moral compass is calling you out on your bad character, and you are not living true to yourself.

Here are twenty-four common traits that define good character. Consider what would be the opposite trait to each sentence, and which side of the aisle do you find yourself living most of the time?

1. *Integrity.* Do you live according to a moral standard, and by what standard do you live?
2. *Honest.* Do you speak, act, and live in the truth?
3. *Loyal.* Are you able to commit to a person, project, or team?
4. *Respectful.* Are your words and deeds seen as respectful, and do you gain respect from others?
5. *Responsible.* Do you keep your word, pay your bills, show up on time, and freely apologize?
6. *Humble.* Do you consider the value of others as more important than yourself?
7. *Compassionate.* Do you try to help people who are suffering, lonely, or in need?
8. *Fair.* Do you distribute justice, consequences, and rewards equally?
9. *Forgiving.* Do you accept apologies and let go of grudges easily?
10. *Authentic.* Are you open and transparent, allowing others to know the real you?
11. *Courageous.* Do you face fear and walk through it because it's the right thing to do?
12. *Generous.* Do you give freely of your time, yourself, and your resources?
13. *Persevere.* When facing a challenge, do you press through the difficulty to completion?
14. *Polite.* Do you speak softly, gently, and do your actions come from a quiet soul?
15. *Kind.* Are you open to hugs, gentle touches, and do you smile often?
16. *Loving.* Do you show love in your words, your actions, and through giving time to others?
17. *Optimistic.* Do you see the good in others, even when they don't see the good themselves?

18. *Reliable.* Do you keep your word, show up on time, and keep your promises?
19. *Conscientious.* Are you aware of another's feelings?
20. *Self-discipline.* Do you control your actions, your words, and your anger?
21. *Ambitious.* Do you take action to improve your life and the life of others?
22. *Encourage.* Do you speak words that lift others up, move them forward, or make them believe in themselves?
23. *Considerate.* Do you look at another's situation and offer ways you may help?
24. *Thorough.* Do you assess what you've accomplished and look for other ways to improve?

As you can see, these words require action, and that action must be done intentionally. We should return to teaching these words to our children. We should be displaying them in our homes. Instead, these words have lost their value and have been replaced by words that do not promote excellence but instead strive for *equality*. How can everyone be considered the same, with equal rewards, and be unique and different at the same time? Can we be both good and bad, weak and strong, equal and exceptional? I don't believe so. When you look at the list, how many of these character traits are rooted in selfish ambition? None. They are all focused on the good of others, how you present yourself, and how you see others as more worthy than yourself. It is rooted in service to others. If you want to be a person of excellent character, you must stop thinking from the perspective of what you want and realize good character is the gift you give others.

Work

Character is best seen in our work ethic. During the 2020 riots and reframing of society's norms, expectations in the work-place changed drastically. Employers were expected to give an hourly wage increase, simply because the government felt they should. The employee was not expected to do anything different. No expectation was allowed that employees increase productivity or work longer hours; they only had to show up and get paid more. Then the pandemic hit. Work stopped, and people were sent home where they received (in some cases) more money for staying home than they did for going to work. This created a mindset where people felt entitled to receive more pay for doing less. Unfortunately, the more money they made, they were moved into a higher tax bracket. They lost their free health insurance, food stamps, and their cost of living suddenly skyrocketed. When inflation hit hard in 2022, the average low-income family ended up with less money at the end of the month than they had before the pay raises.

Additionally, rent moratoriums were created during the pandemic so people wouldn't lose their homes when their jobs were suspended. The property owner had no option as renters refused to pay rent, and the financial burden fell to the landlord. Many renters who lost their jobs (or quit) did not save the money received through government assistance programs and spent it on useless things purchased online in an effort to feel better about themselves. The next year (2021), people lost that financial incentive and landlords could once again ask for rents and they expected all the unpaid rents. Families who were unprepared for the accumulated bills now faced eviction. Some landlords put their homes up for sale to profit from the elevated home prices. Rental property became scarce and rents too expensive that many families were forced to return to the homes of their parents. Others who could find work got jobs in an effort to keep their homes, put food on the table, and gas in their cars. Unfortunately, many more waited for the government to rescue them, and they are still waiting.

Older people were forced out of retirement back into the workforce in order to aid their unemployed, homeless adult children and grandchildren. Fixed incomes did not allow them to keep up with the increased and inflated cost of living. At a time when university graduates were entering the workforce for the first time, desirable jobs were being snatched up by more experienced people, and student loans compounded as good-paying jobs were no longer available. The sandwich generation who is caring for their elderly parents is now also responsible for their adult children and their children. Four and five generations are now living under the same roof in an effort to compile their monies to make ends meet. Crowded together, families are feeling the financial pinch, and relationships are struggling under the pressure of close proximity. Add to this a difference of opinion politically or concerning the vaccine mandates and mask mandates, some families are reaching their boiling point.

A job may not bring you happiness, but the paycheck can be used to purchase things that make you happy. If you love your home and family and want to give to them, a job helps you do that. If you desire a nice car, expensive shoes, or a new set of clubs, a job helps you pay for them. The job may not bring you happiness, but you are not a prisoner because you work. You get to leave at the end of your workday. Maybe you should look outside of your job for the things that make you happy. The job keeps a roof over your head, gas in your car, and food on the table. Happiness is created by you for you. Like the song says, "Don't worry. Be happy," because you can.

> *The aim of psychoanalysis is to relieve people of their neurotic unhappiness so that they can be normally unhappy.* (Sigmund Freud)

Content

Many people have found themselves stuck in this chaotic, challenging position are coming to therapy to address children's behavioral problems, addictions, or unexpected divorce. They express concern for their families and fear for their children's futures. They feel trapped in a situation not of their making and have no idea how to change the outcome. They want to be happy and fear they never will.

In psychology, there is a theory of practice called the Socratic Method attributed to the Greek philosopher Socrates. He taught his students (Plato was one) that we need to debate an idea or concept in order to find the flaw in one's thinking and beliefs. The term *psychology* has its roots in the word *psyche*, or soul, which we translate to "mind." What we believe is our truth. It settles in our mind, and we can believe it to our very *soul*. When we believe an untruth, it also is our truth, and many have fought for a lie only later to find they were wrong. A person's belief of who they are is not determined by how many "friends" you have on social media or your parents' perception of you, and your high school grades speak very little of your ability to perform a task. Your grades should reflect your ability to learn, but with the ability to steal information from the internet, grades alone are not a true reflection of a person's character.

Socrates also defined the concept of happiness. To Socrates, to steal did not bring happiness, but happiness was the satisfaction gained through acquiring by honest means. In other words, if you want to be happy at work, you must be happy with your own production, your contribution, and your ability to learn. Your happiness comes from knowing you are doing a good job, showing up on time, and that you bring value to the workplace. Your employer's and coworker's praise should not be the only thing that makes you happy. If you do not receive constant praise (and most people don't get daily doses of it), you will be miserable and will blame the job, your employer, your spouse, or your circumstances for your misery.

Happiness is not something that is sustainable because it is dependent on your outlook, your circumstance, and your expectations all being in alignment with a positive experience and outcome. When anything prohibits that alignment from occurring, you feel unhappy. You will resent the person or object that is preventing you from being happy and often will seek other means of being happy, even if they are destructive and damaging to yourself or your relationships.

Instead of seeking to be happy, seek contentment. People who are content realize they can choose how to respond to situations and not just react to them. When you experience a challenge, even difficulty, you can still feel content as this is a personal choice. People of character realize their contentment is not determined by other people, their place of employment, or their financial status. They can have no money, no possessions, no job, and no home, and yet they can be content where they are. They learn to be content by appreciating the things they have and not focusing on what they don't have.

Gratitude leads us to be content. When we know every breath we have is a gift, we can receive it with a happy heart.

For the Spirit God gave us does not make us timid, but gives us power, love and self-discipline. (2 Timothy 1:7 NIV)

CHAPTER 5

Intentional Presence

*Who is wise and understanding among you? Let
them show it by their good life, by deeds done
in the humility that comes from wisdom.*

—James 3:13 (NIV)

When I think of what it is to be intentionally present, I think
it is the awareness of oneself within one's environment; in
other words, who you are in relation to your home, your school, your
work, and your relationships. When you know who you are in all the
roles you represent (mother/father, daughter/son, wife/husband, sibling, employee, student, etc.), you can make individual, intentional
decisions that benefit you and everyone around you. When you don't
know who you are or what your role is in your environment, you can
become paralyzed and immobile while you wait for others to define
you. When this happens, the definitions are usually not to benefit
you but to benefit the one who is labeling you:

- A parent can call you "a burden."
- A sibling can call you "loser."
- A teacher can call you "lazy."
- An employer can call you "unmotivated."
- A society can call you "a hindrance."

So many people in society have become unable to live, think, or function independently. They were never taught to think for themselves and so need others to think for them. They don't know how to work because the work has always been done for them. They don't know how to change because they were never challenged to change. They don't know how to solve problems because they were never taught to think in terms of critical thinking when applied to their own lives. Yet those same people who have no idea how to live their own lives are the same people who are telling others how they should live. People used to couch surf in their parent's living rooms, but now the couches have moved out of the home and into the field, onto the beach, and created political and emotional landfills.

As we've discussed, to live your best life, you must be intentional, and this includes your environment. If you surround yourself with fools, you will be one of them. If you surround yourself with people who praise academia, you will be intellectual, but you might not have any wisdom. If you surround yourself with greedy people, you will be a liar, cheat, and a thief. If you surround yourself with addicts and drunks, you will be wasting your life away.

The opposite is true as well. If you surround yourself with good-hearted people who are generous, kind, caring, and loving, you will learn how to acquire those things as well. But watching isn't being. Notice I said "acquire"? This means you must work at learning and applying the gifts they offer you. It takes work, courage, and patience to learn how to be a good person. It doesn't take much effort at all to learn how to be selfish. Even a baby knows how to do that because it's in our nature. To gain wisdom, you have to fight against the lies of acceptance. To work hard, you must fight against laziness. To be honest, you must fight against selfishness. To be loving, you must fight against indifference. To be fair, you must fight against revenge. We can all get crazy with the many challenges of today. Take it a day at a time and plan your steps to get you where you want to go.

As a therapist and business developer, one of the best parts of working with teams of unique and very diverse therapists is we get to learn about each other's dreams, desires, challenges, and accomplishments. Recently, while I was surrounded by my team for our weekly supervision and training session, one of my therapists shared a story of her childhood that was both touching and encouraging.

The topic for the day's lesson was on the difference between *authentic*, *real*, and *true*. As usual for the group, all were engaged in a lively exchange of ideas, understandings, and personal experiences that supported each offered concept. Sylvia, who had recently graduated with her master's degree, shared her personal story of learning how to embrace her gift of singing. Sylvia was a contestant on both *The Voice* and *American Idol*. This was the first time I had heard this, and to further impress us, she sang a song her grandmother taught her as a young girl. She began the song with a soft and low voice, but by the end of the song she was belting out the words with energy that gave the rest of us a truly magical experience. That day, the words and the story behind Sylvia's discovery of a gift that has blessed her through the years truly blessed us all.

These are the lyrics to "I Am a Promise" written by Bill and Gloria Gaither:

I am a Promise
I am a Possibility
I am a Promise
With a capital P
I am a great big bundle of Potentiality
And I am learning
To hear God's voice
And I am trying
To make the right choice
I am a Promise to Be
Anything he wants me to be!

Sylvia's parting perspective was, "When you know who you are in the eyes of the Lord, you can be and do anything because anything is possible." I wholeheartedly agree.

Perspective

There are more and more people today who are quitting life. I'm not talking about the ones who commit suicide; albeit, that is the ultimate form of quitting. I'm talking about the walking dead, the ones who have no reason to live, but they continue to breathe. They get up every day, go to work or school, learn, make money, and return home. They have low energy, so even when they are present with others, they are not engaged. They may be married and have children, but their existence lacks awareness. They can be sitting in a room filled with trash and would never even think to put anything in the garbage. There can be a screaming baby nearby, and they wouldn't even hear him. Their spouse yells trying to motivate them, yet they stare into space. Children may pull on their sleeve begging for attention, but they look into their little eyes and feel nothing. They are the walking dead among us, and as a nation, we are creating a generation of zombies.

Whatever you focus on will be your perspective, and that perspective creates your reality. When you find others in opposition to your perspective, you shouldn't fight against them but try to understand them. When you see truth and evidence to support it, you will know your perspective is accurate. When people insist on holding on to a lie, you can be sure they are gaining something from it.

Consider how, post pandemic, children have suffered psychologically more than the virus ever could have harmed them. Many were forced to stay home with critical, perfectionistic parents who were never trained how to be teachers. After two years of disappointment and feeling defeated at every turn, many became debilitated and stopped trying. They learned to cope by playing video games, smoking pot, drinking, and watching porn. In some cases, they have no clue how to change and don't believe anything can change. So they take a gun to school and kill anyone who bullied them. During the 2020 to 2021 pandemic, 22.3 percent more children ended up in hospitals from attempting to commit suicide. Many turned the guns on themselves and end the agony they never should have endured.

Yet some parents are so eager to return to their own routines and sense of normalcy they blindly will send their children back into the battle to fight the war alone. Other parents who feel they want to protect their children keep them home. In all cases, the children and parents were not prepared for all the rapid-fire changes that left us feeling confused and out of control. Conversely, when you consider the winds of change, where they begin, and to what purpose they serve, you can see the truth of the situation and adapt. When you know where you are going, you can plan ahead, make any necessary course corrections, prepare, and adapt for the next coming storm.

Since the pandemic, our office has been flooded with families who have suffered the loss of a loved one. Children who lost one parent are acting out as the remaining parent grieves or, worse yet, avoids grief by distracting themselves with work or unhealthy relationships. The children literally scream for attention, and the parent who is blinded by their inability to see beyond their own grief feels at a loss to help. One such parent brought her ten-year-old daughter in for therapy because she was "acting out," and the parent didn't know how to control her anymore.

When sharing their story, the mother said, "She needs to get over the loss of her father. He's dead, and he's not coming back." She proudly admitted she had moved on from the loss of her partner and was dating several men in an effort to find a new "daddy" for her daughter.

The girl shared her father had hung himself in their garage, and she had found him. How was this girl going to just move on? The solution was the family needed to find a way to adapt to their circumstances without letting them cause further destruction and harm.

Adaptability

When a child experiences the loss of one parent to death, divorce, or separation, they do not have the ability to just disconnect like most adults wish they could. A child does not experience the relationship with their parents in the same way couples do. For a parent who has grown distant and cold toward their spouse or partner, it has taken place over months and even years. But the child is not present in *that* relationship. They are involved in their own relationship with their parent. A parent who expects a child to be angry with a parent who has cheated on them is unrealistic. The parent did not cheat on the child, and their relationship has not changed. The hurt parent tries to align the child to their side looking for comfort, and the child is dragged into the conflict against their will. The younger the child, the less their ability to discern what is happening. The older the child, they may be aware of their parent's discord and by choice avoids getting involved. No one in the middle of a crisis is able to be present for the rest of the family as each focus on their own immediate needs. The parents are unable to see the forest (hope) for the trees (challenges) that stand in their way.

When you begin to live intentionally, to think with an open mind, to hear with ears willing to listen, and to see clearly what is and not what you want to see, you'll begin to realize that you have choices in the decisions you make. In most cases, you can see a clear choice of right versus wrong, good versus bad, blessings versus curses. But what about the times when the decisions are not that clear when you don't have a good choice but only bad options? How do you move forward when no direction will take you where you want to go? That's the moment when you determine to make the choice to be intentionally present.

> *Who will rise up for me against the wicked?*
> *Who will take a stand for me against evildoers?*
> (Psalm 94:16 NIV)

CHAPTER 6

Intentional Choices

*Fools find no pleasure in understanding but
delight in airing their own opinions.*
—Proverbs 18:2 (NIV)

Many of today's youth don't know who they are. They have no goals, no ambition, and no objectivity about the life they live. They look around at others and wonder why they don't fit in. Fitting in is paramount in their world, and acceptance is all they desire. Because it's all they strive for, it becomes the only measurement for any accomplishment. Those who have no direction look for a cause that they can rally behind and stand beside others who would embrace them as one of their own. They may not even understand why the rally is taking place. It's not really the focus of the rally that they participate in but the inclusion with those who have passion, energy, and ambition that they themselves do not possess. It's as if they were desiring to absorb the energy from others so that they might feel alive in an otherwise world that is dead. But what happens when the crowd disperses, and they go home alone? Who is there to give them the energy they need to get out of bed when for three days, they couldn't muster the energy on their own? Who is there to pull them from the darkness that makes them depressed? Who is there to distract them from the panic attack that lurks in the back of their mind? Who is there to tell them that they are proud of you, that they believe in them, and that they want to be your friend? Who is there when no one else is there? This is the question of a generation who has learned helplessness as a way of life.

Across America and the world, there are more people who have become dependent in one way or another. They rely upon others to house and feed them, yet homelessness continues to increase. They insist on higher wages, while those who are willing to work for less take their jobs. They are willing to comply with every mandate because they only know how to comply. They fear losing the portion they receive, even though that portion does not provide enough. They cannot stand on their own as generational dependence is all they know. Others have left poverty to become independent, successful, and even rich. Why do the ones who have the ability to lift others up keep them locked in dependence?

Influence

When someone doesn't feel your legacy has value, they feel justified to snuff it out. In all cases where someone forfeits their choices to another, they place themselves in a situation of vulnerability. Sometimes we are vulnerable because of our circumstances that limit us. We can be born into poverty, live in a city filled with crime, and may have experienced trauma from an early age. Our limited resources create limited opportunity, and that furthers our dependence and vulnerability. The cycle repeats as our unmet needs run into limited resources that do not allow for those needs to be met. So we must look outside of ourselves and our circumstances to find someone who can help. Once we find that person, we put ourselves under their control in order to receive our basic needs. The person who is helping does not do this for free, and they begin to make demands. The more they demand, restrict, and manipulate the other, the more the other feels vulnerable and incapable of taking care of themselves and become more dependent.

When someone is dependent on another for financial, emotional, or physical support, it is easy to become vulnerable to the other's manipulation and control. Reliance upon another means forfeiting self-reliance, and in some cases, abuse can occur. The dependent person can fall into despair and hopelessly implode in a pool of depression, experiencing panic attacks whenever they feel vulnerable or at risk. Fear consumes their minds, so they can't even think as emotions determine all choices. Nothing good comes from making choices while in this heightened state of emotional dysregulation.

Today, most people are living in a constant state of stress. They are existing in a survival state of mind most of the time. They think and react to emotions that drive subconscious behaviors that become the basis of their existence and wonder why they do what they do. Most decisions made from a place of fear are not intentional as they are driven by pure emotion. When we make choices without intent, we are making illogical decisions. When we make intentional choices, we are making decisions logically.

Codependency

Entire books are written on this subject, and my goal is not to write another book on the topic of codependency. Having said that, we are relational beings, and as such, we can interact with others in healthy and unhealthy ways. Fear often leads us to assume the thoughts of another person, and we try to meet their unspoken needs without them even saying a word. We might pick up on some negative energy, a look or body language that reminds us of another person, place, or time when we failed to meet someone's expectations, and it resulted in negative consequences. There are many problems with this approach to meeting someone's unspoken need. First, you don't know for certain if this is really a need of theirs. Secondly, you don't know if it's what they are needing right now. If you give (time, money, sex, etc.) in an effort to meet a need they are not expecting you to meet, it can feel controlling and manipulative. During an argument is not the time to give flowers, money, or other *gifts* in an effort to end conflict. When you assume someone will meet your expectations, remember: unless the other person knows what your expectations are, they are unspoken and will remain unrealized. When you go back and recap what happened, you may discover your good intentions were truly an unconscious attempt to manipulate the other to giving you what you wanted. You gave not to meet their need but to meet your own needs: the need for peace, connection, and appreciation. And when you didn't get it, you became angry and resentful.

Let's take that same situation and make an intentional choice. You have a feeling someone is upset with you because you are being triggered by their words, their actions, a look, or their body language. You ask them, "Is everything okay? I'm feeling a weird vibe, and I'm not sure if you're upset with me." The other person tells you they have something on their mind, and that it has nothing to do with you. You ask if there is something they need from you, "Do you want to talk about it?" They begin to share their concerns, and you listen. When they are finished, you give them a hug, encourage them, and offer advice if they ask. They appreciate your offer, you feel connected, and you have peace. The other felt heard and was able to verbally process their concern with you. You both had your needs met at the same time because your choice was intentional.

When you focus on something from a place of fear, you will manifest that thing you fear. When you believe in possibility, you will find that manifested in your life. The automatic negative thinking that leads to reactive emotional choices causes most conflict. Our emotions drive poor choices rooted in fears that something bad will happen. In an effort to feel better, we make the bad choice, but then the resulting consequences often end in self-fulfilling prophecy where we reinforce the negative thoughts, and the pattern continues to agnosia. Only by stopping the negative thoughts driven by fear and standing in truth, confidence, and making a decision that is rooted in logical thinking can we make intentional choices.

Recently, there have been a lot of blank stares looking back at me when I ask young people what they are looking for in a relationship. They have no idea how beneficial it might be to look for a *type* of person rather than just "fall" into relationships as easily as they fall into bed. They resort to sex as the measure for compatibility and break up when they are no longer compatible. They were never truly compatible in the first place. Sleeping with someone you know nothing about is not the way to developing a relationship. I told a young lady who allowed someone to press upon her their intentions that she was experiencing a false sense of guilt. She stopped him before it went too far, but she felt responsible for his actions. I explained that she was not responsible for his behaviors, only her response to his behaviors. I explained she can be motivated by *influence* (lead a horse to water) and set strong boundaries when she recognizes *manipulation* when it is happening. Don't allow anyone to force you into doing something you don't want to do, even if it hurts their feelings. Be strong, be confident, and know that you have a choice. Just say *no*!

Addiction

There are all kinds of addiction, and we are a society who enjoys and flaunts our addictions with pride. We celebrate life in our addiction even while we slowly die. We drink, smoke, eat, gamble, and lust for our addictions. Sometimes we are so addicted to the mere feeling of being addicted that to consider a life without our addiction is unthinkable.

I recommended a gentleman turn off his news feeds after he reported increased anxiety and depression. Every conversation we had was a recounting of all the negative things he had heard in his social media feed, his conversation with friends, or what he heard in the news. He was addicted to hearing negative talk and couldn't figure out why he was consumed with negative thinking. When he eliminated the negative static in his life, even though it was hard for him to turn it off, he reported within weeks that his depression and anxiety were so much better he was able to stop taking his medication. I wish everyone would turn off the negative and seek to live in the positive. You can stop the flood of negative thinking that you allow into your mind. Flip the switch, push the button, and close the window of negativity you crave. All it takes is a little effort, determination, and a choice. The same mind that makes the choice to turn it on can also choose to turn it off.

Alcohol consumption and therapy do not go well together. Alcohol denies culpability, and therapy reveals the truth. As long as this dance continues, therapy is not happening, and healing cannot occur. For an alcoholic to have a chance to reach any level of healthy functioning, they must address the elephant in the room, their addiction. So often, that same elephant must sit on the addict's head before they feel the pressure to change, and sometimes the crushing effects are fatal.

By the time someone comes to couples or family therapy for help with failed relationships, homelessness, or self-harm ideation, they have been rooted in their addiction for years, decades, or even a lifetime. The journey to sobriety may take just as long as it takes to travel through the process of recovery and repair. The two go hand in hand if forgiveness and trust are to be rebuilt. This can only happen if the alcoholic (or addict) is willing to stop the drinking games and get serious with the battle that lay ahead. There will be fear, there will be failures, and there will be a desire to quit. Yes, these things will consume your thoughts, and they may be a part of your life for as long as you live. But assuredly, if you press through the triggers, the cravings, and the many reasons why you feel justified to drink (or use), you will find courage waiting on the other side of the fear. Do it every day, several times a day, and you may find you've traveled so much further than you ever believed you could because if you believe you can…you will.

I have worked with people caught up in addiction for years—and they are a tough bunch to help change. Until they feel like changing, they won't. They must accept that they have a problem first, or they will not seek help and will return to their addiction over and over again.

Addiction, of all types, comes on gradually, by the glass, the pill, a photo, and doesn't stop until it's got a death grip around your neck and is strangling the life out of you. Most addicts won't feel like changing until everything around them has been lost, and they have nothing more to lose. For many, only death will stop their addiction.

You don't believe me? Look at the homeless problem for example. It's reported the number one and two causes of homelessness are *addiction* and *mental health* respectively. Look at the breakup of relationships. The main cause of breakups is pornography, deception, and unfaithfulness. Look at most relationships and you'll see selfishness, abuse, addiction, and narcissistic behaviors at the root of their problems.

When people get *hooked* on some object (drugs, alcohol, porn, food) or a place (gym, extreme sports, work, church, hobbies) or people (codependent relationships, political figures, or the rich and famous), they become "addicted" to the person, place, or thing. The person, place, or object starts running the show, and they are just "going along for the ride." When a group of people get together to enjoy their addiction, the purpose for the group may not be negative. A group can be comprised of people who attend church together under the same faith, attend the same university, or athletes and spectators who gather for events and competitions. But it can also be people who have a common desire to undermine society's norms, remove safety valves, and destroy past protections. The world is changing so rapidly in the aftermath of 2020 that people are reaching for anything that will make them feel good, feel distracted, or just want something to feel other than fear.

Feelings

We give way too much power to our feelings. Emotions are not facts, and when we think our feelings are flawless, we can make unrealistic demands of others. Feelings come and go and can be impacted by something as simple as hunger, lust, or fear. Our thoughts drive our feelings, and if we think negatively toward someone, we will feel negative toward them as well. When we want to feel different and can't shut off the negative thoughts, the bottle, the video, or the joint seem like a great way to turn down the noise in our minds. Unfortunately, this only prolongs the pain, and suffering continues. There is help and hope for those who seek it.

Change

Change is always happening. It can happen to you without your permission, and it can happen intentionally. Change can be experience as good or bad (positive or negative). Change can manifest slowly over a lifetime or in a moment in time. Change happens to us, with us, and for us. Change can happen with the altering of a perspective, a color, or a space. It can be a smile, a frown, or an unexpected laugh. It can be positive or negative. It can be a blessing or a curse. You can see it coming and make plans to drive it, or it can catch you unexpectantly. It can be the gentle touch of a newborn or hit you like a freight train in the middle of the night. You cannot change your past, but you can certainly plan to change your future. Change makes you look inward, outward, and sideways with suspicion at another's actions. It can make you jealous, fearful, and dreading the morning light. It can bring shame, guilt, and horror when you look at the changes you made. Change also can bring joy, faith, and hope. We cannot plan for all areas where change resides, but we can be aware that change is inevitable.

FOO

In psychosocial assessments, there is always a section for Family of Origin (FOO). This is usually an area of contention and must be considered when diagnosing for mental disorders. Holidays can bring out the best and worst qualities of families, and FOO issues are revealed like the stomping of reindeer's feet on the roofs of our souls.

There is a Christmas song that says, "It's the most wonderful time of the year!" But for many, it's the most painful time of the year. Family dysfunction is magnified by unrealistic expectations, followed by unfair judgments, resulting in compounding guilt and shame. Sometimes, we don't realize as adults we have the right to make choices how we want to deal with family during the holidays. Most of the time, we see the holidays coming and try to avoid how we feel. Then one day, we get the dreaded phone call inviting us to the family gathering, and unprepared with a reasonable excuse, we accept. After we hang up, the fears begin to build as we are reminded of prior holidays that ended poorly or in family conflict.

Some people say they feel obligated to attend a family gathering but hate the idea of entering an unsafe environment. Some people fear abuse of the past being repeated in the present and don't know how to avoid it. Others know they have a choice but are compelled to attend because they *hope* this year will be different from the past. There's an old saying that goes "misery loves company," and it's so true when it comes to dysfunctional holiday gatherings. Many families like to "catch up" on the judgments they were not able to pour on another family member all the rest of the year. Maybe they heard rumors from another family member, parent, or siblings. They judge the other's behaviors and shame them in front of the rest of the family. They bring up past hurts and demand restitution. They use the time of gathering as a time to clear the air instead of a time to celebrate each other.

Find a way or find an excuse.
Be responsible or be a victim.
Either way, it's your choice.

When my clients tell me they are afraid, anxious, and depressed because of the upcoming family gathering, I advise them to have a plan before they get the invitation to dinner. Here are a couple of examples how to set boundaries to avoid the holiday tradition of dysfunction.

It's okay to say "No, thank you" when a family member invites you to their home if you believe your time there will be negative. If you are asked why you can't attend, add the next line.

It's okay to say "I have other plans" and not explain what those plans are, even if they are to stay at home with a TV dinner and watch football. Often, we overexplain, and then it becomes an argument as they attempt to manipulate and guilt us into attending. Stay calm and just repeat yourself, then say you must go now. Hang up if they continue to insist.

It's okay to say, "Thank you. Yes, I'll be there, but I have to leave by 2:00." By setting a limit to the time you are exposed to others is an effective escape plan. You can stay longer if the time is pleasant, but you can leave when it's not.

It's okay to ask if a family member who you have difficulty with will be there. If they are, offer an alternative day to get with the host (Christmas Day versus Christmas Eve). If they want a family photo with everyone there, offer to come for the photo, but say you won't stay beyond that. If the offensive person attempts to engage you, give your apologies to the host and leave. Don't stay and engage in conflict that someone else is starting. Walk away.

When you are prepared for problems you anticipate, you can make a plan to avoid them. First, ask yourself what you want. Once you know what you want, it becomes easier to offer alternative options or solutions to avoid conflict. If you want to stay and enjoy a meal with family, then do so. If someone is creating conflict or trying to start an argument, you can have options to leave already prepared. You can simply choose not to remain, and remaining because you feel obligated only creates resentment. What you give of yourself during the holidays is determined by your choices. You can give of your time, money, and love and have no expectation of others to give in return. By realizing that what you give is an unconditional gift, you free yourself from needing anything in return. When you give with an expectation to receive something, a gift, love, or admiration, you are giving conditionally and will be hurt when your expectations are not met. Determine what you will give, then give it freely. Only you determine the value of the gift. If you want to give a small gift or large one, give it freely. If you want to give a couple hours of your time or the whole day, give it freely. If you want to give love, then give it without expectation that you will receive anything back.

Here are a few truisms to live or die by; the choice is yours. You can't

- Demand independence and remain dependent;
- Gain wealth by refusing to work;
- Demand control while giving away power;
- Avoid death by forfeiting life,
- Demand of others what you won't do yourself;
- Get rich by decreasing the wealth of others;
- Grow while avoiding change;

- Live in truth while embracing a lie;
- Live free by choosing submission.

Always live your life in control of your choices. When you have the right to choose what you will and won't give, whatever you give, give it freely. Understand that when you have the power to decide, the consequences are also yours to receive. Don't make poor decisions, then force others to suffer the consequences. Your choice, your responsibility. Your power, your control. Your problem, solve it. And always remember, when you change, everything changes.

> *When you get into a tight place and everything goes against you, till it seems you cannot hold on a minute longer, never give up then, for that is just the place and time the tide will turn.* (Harriet Beecher Stowe)

CHAPTER 7

Intentional Love

*The beginning of wisdom is this: Get wisdom. Though
it cost all you have, get understanding.*
—Proverbs 4:7 (NIV)

Isn't love grand? I mean, really. Someone touches your hand, and you look into their eyes and *wham*, it's meant to be. You know it's love for certain because you both like the same sandwich, drive similar cars, sort of, and enjoy the same types of things, except for football. You can do without all that sports stuff. But he's whispered tender sweet nothings in your ears till they dripped in honey (yuck). He's poured all his money into impressing you with expensive gifts that you don't need, flowers that make your allergies flare up, chocolates that add twenty pounds to your hips, and romantic getaways that leave you paying off credit cards for years. Heck, who wouldn't want to be in love? And then consider that if you fell in love so quickly, you may just as easily fall out of love, looking for the next touch, look, or song that will make you swoon and fall again.

Oh brother! So let's look at reality…

What is love? If you compared love through the ages, you would find love in many different forms. Some people spent entire lives together, raised children, and supported each other in the name of love, but no love exited between them. Mostly, what they felt was obligation and fear of judgment if they didn't stay together. Some people stayed together "for the sake of the kids" and found ways to coexist until the children were old enough to "understand" why Mommy and Daddy couldn't live together anymore. Some people stayed together because of a mutual understanding regarding finances, housing, or for some other convenience. Some people stayed with someone for image only. They liked the way love looked on them, but they didn't really want to buy it. Some people wanted the feeling of love but were unwilling to invest in the work it took to keep love alive. Some people had arranged marriages where they met their betrothed for the first time on their wedding day. Others knew their partners for years before they wed only to realize later, they were complete strangers.

And then there are the few who get it right, and they have a love that lasts a lifetime…right? No. They realized that love is not a feeling but a decision they make to love another despite how they felt about them. They determined to commit to the other "until death do us part."

To live your best life, you must be intentional, and this includes your love life. Everyone who considers what they want in any relationship first says they want to be loved. The challenge is finding someone who shares the same definition of love that you do (review the previous chapter). When we enter a new relationship, any relationship, we must learn who we are individually as well as who they are to us. We are learning a new dance with a new partner, yet we must dance the same dance if we are to continue to dance at all. Otherwise, it's a dance-floor fight.

No one can dance with a partner and not touch each other's "raw spots."

We must know what these raw spots are and be able to speak about them in a way that pulls our partner closer to us. I think, ultimately, hurt will come. We can't dance in close proximity without occasionally stepping on each other's toes.

However, love, like a dance, is a constant process of tuning in, connecting, missing and misreading cues, disconnecting, repairing, and finding deeper connection. It is a dance of meeting and parting and finding each other again, minute to minute and day to day. Just learning to dance more gracefully over time and gaining experience means committing to being on the dance floor every day, paying attention, and attuning to the music, steps, and emotions of your partner. When you find your rhythm and can glide across the dance floor of time, you may find yourself ending the song in eternity.

Round pegs, square holes

The subject of love always comes up in therapy during the month of February and especially as Valentine's Day approaches. I hear the same complaint, "It's nearly impossible to find a compatible partner today." One of my clients told me, "I've tried to date, but nothing seems to feel right. We just don't click." I have empathy for the challenges that young adults are facing with high expectations, few dating options, and unclear gender roles due to living in a world where gender identity is fluid. There are so many obstacles to finding love that many give up and settle for a life of discouraged singleness.

This is unacceptable and unnecessary.

When I work with singles, I have them identify why they want to date. Is it for love or lust that they look? Many who have a skewed idea of love think these terms are one and the same. But they are very different. Love requires a desire for a commitment. Lust requires only attraction. Love grows over time as you build a deep connection. Lust is shallow, quick, and over just as fast as it started. Love requires intention, grace, and forgiveness. Lust doesn't require anything, and you can quit for any reason. Most people don't realize they are approaching love with a lust focus hoping it will turn into love. Unfortunately, this hope seldom is realized. Lust, by definition, is not love and can never become love. When you build a relationship that is shallow to begin with, it's difficult to go any deeper once the focus has been on sex and lust. You may grow to have a commitment, but usually, it's not love that drives the commitment but children or a reluctance to change. Those who pursue love, where people focus on building a relationship first and setting sex to the side, experience a more meaningful relationship that develops slowly over time. People who are impatient to find love end up in cycles of lust that continue to frustrate them. These people are the ones who say, "All the good ones are taken." It takes patience to find love. You can't treat the person you want to love like the person you lust after as they will leave feeling unfulfilled. When you take time to look into the eyes of the one you love, you see them. When you look only at someone's body as a target for conquest, the person remains unseen.

The person today who wants to find love and not just fulfil lust must be willing to face rejection as you may be looking for love with others who are only seeking to fulfil their lust. When I showed the aforementioned gentleman that he was searching for a place to put his "round peg," and he was discouraged with only finding all the "square holes" because they were easy, he accepted settling for lust because it required little commitment from him. It also meant there was little to no risk of failure or rejection. His frustration climaxed when he realized he needed to look for the girls with the "round holes" who would match his ideals of love. When he saw the drawing on the whiteboard that reflected this concept, he had an *aha* moment. He was looking for love in all the wrong places, with all the wrong girls, and with the wrong focus.

When you don't know what you're looking for, it's easy to find.

Fight

I encourage couples to fight. Yes, I know, most couples don't need a lot of coaxing to fight; they can do it all on their own. They fight for the wrong reasons, with the wrong goals, and the wrong methods. They fight because they are hurt, frustrated, or afraid that they made a poor choice in their mate. They think they know what they are fighting about but have no clue what started the fight in the first place. They are confused, overwhelmed, and exhausted with trying to be understood. They want to win the battle, to be proven correct, and they strive to be vindicated of any wrongdoing. They have selfish intentions, have a lack of concern for their partner's feelings, and feel justified when accused of being hurtful or unfair. These couples fight, but they fight wrong.

The most successful couples are the ones who have learned to fight correctly. I love working with couples who truly want to improve their relationship. Do they fight? Yes! But they will listen to ways to fight fair. Do they get angry? Yes! But once they understand the reasons for their anger (hurt, fear, frustration), they can adjust their responses instead of defending them. Do they feel like leaving sometimes and never coming back? Yes! There is nothing wrong with taking a break, going for a walk, and taking a deep breath before returning to apologize, to clarify, and to forgive.

These couples are willing to listen before they seek to be understood. They want what is best for their partner and want them to be happy above all else. They are sacrificial in their giving, and they compete to show the most love for each other. They fight for their love, for their relationship, and for their future. They never give up, tire, or threaten to walk away. They know each other's insecurities, and they strive to protect those vulnerabilities, not take advantage of them. They understand that war takes a lot of effort and energy, and the longer the battle, the more they need to take time out. These couples feel safe to share their ideas, their concerns, and their fears. They trust their partner to apologize and repair any damage they may have caused during the argument. There is never any intention of abuse, and even though words can sometimes hurt, they always desire to speak the truth wrapped up in love.

Commitment

Many people don't understand what a commitment is or see the value in committing to something. They can't commit to finishing a movie, a course, or a project before they get up and walk out of the theatre, school, or job. Everyone is looking for immediate gratification, and positive feelings are the measurement for success in their relationships. "As long as you make me happy, I'll stay. The minute you make me unhappy, I'm out." Why do people get so upset when the other makes the same statement and walks out first? When there is no commitment by either side, there is no right to have an expectation they would stay. When you jump into a relationship, it's only natural to jump out of it.

These same people jump out of relationships for all kinds of reasons too. They can quit a relationship because they got bored, tired, or realized what they thought was love was really just a one-night-stand kind of love, not the stay-for-all-time kind of love. They can see someone else who catches their eye, their attention, or makes their loins flutter. It can be for the simplest of reasons or no reason at all. When people don't commit, they are already telling you that you are temporary. The only ones who stay are the ones who haven't found a good enough reason to leave. Yet.

This kind of sucks, I know. But I work in the world of reality and not fantasy. I'm not writing a romance novel. I'm trying to give you a wake-up call. If you are tired of the repeated insanity of start-and-stop relationships and want a better way to finding Mr., Mrs., or Ms. Right, then you have to stop shopping in the shoe store and trying on every shoe looking for the one that "feels right." When I go hiking, I buy a hiking boot. When I go dancing, I wear appropriate shoes for the dance. When I run, walk, or ride my horse, I wear the shoe that best serves the need.

Relationships work the same way. Know what you want a relationship for first, then find a person who wants that kind of relationship too. If you are looking for lust, that's pretty easy to fill. It doesn't require a whole lot of knowledge about the person you plan to have sex with. Just get a blood test and be safe about your decision. If you want to date for the sake of dating and not for love, then let the other person know this from the start. Don't deceive and manipulate someone into a lie just so you can get a free meal. Go back to the "Character" chapter if this is who you currently are because that qualifies as "poor character." If you are looking for marriage, and you want children and have a specific dream you want to fulfill, you have to be honest about it; to yourself first, then your potential partner. If you don't know what you want, you'll try to climb a relationship ladder by starting with the least commitment and trying to make it evolve into the top rung of the ladder. This approach seldom works as you'll date someone from the lowest denominator, and they may not want to climb the ladder with you.

Deceivers

Have you ever been deceived by another and wondered why you didn't see it coming? We have an automatic defense mechanism that is built in that helps us find what we are looking for. It is a sub-conscious cognitive mechanism that helps us rapidly eliminate things that we are not looking for. Our brain wants to work as quickly and efficiently as possible, and so automatically, it selects what is most pertinent in the moment. Have you ever purchased a car in a particular color thinking it was going to be unique because you've *never* seen this car in that color before? Then you drove off the lot, and suddenly, *everyone* is driving a car just like yours. Our mind will seek out things we expect to see and behaviors we expect to happen and will reframe them to match our beliefs. We make others our enemy, not because of who they are but because of who we are. This creates a barrier to learning the truth and makes finding a solution impossible because the problem is all in your mind. This is called a blind spot, and it is a result of a personal bias we have that holds others to a standard that is of our own making. It also is a higher standard than that to which we hold ourselves. This standard allows the one who set the standard to be both judge and jury to feel more superior to those they judge. It requires no real measurement to justify the punishment for crimes committed against one's psyche.

The final thought is, "I feel hurt. Therefore, you must die."

Conversely, we also can have blind spots when we compare our performance with others and see our weaknesses. We can feel guilt and shame for the things we lack, our inabilities, and emphasize our failures. We see others as perfect, capable, and emphasize their gifts and talents. In both situations, our vision is skewed to the positive or the negative way we view ourselves and others. In reality, there are always going to be things about ourselves and others that we do not see, can't see, or choose not to see. This standard allows the one who set the standard to be both judge and jury to feel *less* superior to those they judge.

The final thought is, "You hurt. Therefore, I must die."

Dr. Tony Evans, pastor of The Urban Alternative, says,

> If all you see, is what you see, then you are not seeing all you can see. Until you see what you can't see, you will not be able to see all that there is to see. Behind everything that you can't see, is something for you to look at that you can't see. For beyond what you see is what you can't see, but what you should be seeing.

To get to know someone takes time, commitment, and an open mind. Often, people would rather judge based on their bias without getting to know the person. Yet, everyone is screaming to be known, to be seen, and to be heard. There is a difference between hurt and harm. During the COVID-19 pandemic, many riots broke out because of perceived social injustices. Years later, the riots, burning of buildings, and destruction of lives have not improved those perceptions, hurt feelings, or remedied the reasons that caused such harm. If what you are looking for is validation, speak to the one who hurt you; don't yell at them. Help them understand you; don't beat them up because they don't. When you give compassion, you'll receive it. When you listen first, others are willing to listen to you. When you speak without hate, you'll most likely receive words that are kinder and less hurtful. When you are the one doing the yelling and making demands, you are ignoring your own blind spots and blaming others. When you can see, hear, and believe what others say, you are open to real understanding.

This approach to understanding also applies to your family members, friends, and acquaintances, but it also applies to how you see God and how you think God sees you.

Compromise

When you are ready to go after what you want in a relationship, don't compromise. Be honest with yourself and the other person, and if you realize you want different things, don't continue the dating relationship. You can remain friendly toward each other, but are you looking for a friend? If not, are they going to really be a friend after you no longer see each other romantically? If you want friends, that's discussed in the next chapter. We're talking love now, and even though we may love our friends, a friend with benefits is not love. When you compromise your goals and dreams, you will resent and regret that decision for many days, weeks, years to come. Compromise makes you feel connected, but it's like hooking your truck up to someone else's trailer. You don't know what's inside until you open the doors and realize it's not filled with the things you thought. When you are certain you have done your best to go after the things you want, and you are certain the other person has your dreams and goals in mind, when they agree to "hook up" their trailer (after you've looked inside of course), you are more likely to get to a common destination where love abounds.

> *But blessed are your eyes because they see, and your ears because they hear.*
> *For truly I tell you, many prophets and righteous people longed to see what you see but did not see it, and to hear what you hear but did not hear it.* (Matthew 13:16–17 NIV)

CHAPTER 8

Intentional Relationships

*Walk with the wise and become wise, for a
companion of fools suffers harm.*
—Proverbs 13:20 (NIV)

Relationships are hard. They are meant to be hard. The only way to grow, to improve, and to become better is to be challenged. The Bible says, "Iron sharpens iron" (Proverbs 27:17), and when we realize we can teach as well as learn, then many blessings will result. Lessons need to be learned in the relationship, and avoiding conflict does nothing to improve your ability to learn. Avoidance keeps you ignorant and unable to clarify your position. Avoidance encourages another to take control. When you refuse to take control of yourself, you force the other person to take responsibility for your choices, which feels good to you as you avoid responsibility but angers the other who must be responsible.

No one wants to be in a relationship with an adult child. The only children in the relationship should be the minor children who *need* you to be in control. It takes two mature adults to create a happy relationship. A healthy partner won't want to be responsible for your actions. When both people have the respect of the other, they can give and take and share the control during an argument, and peace will prevail. The relationship will have a better chance to thrive, and loving feelings will grow between the couple. When you pour into each other so much love it overflows, it fills the cups of those around you, including your children, family, and friends.

Balance

If we don't make time for friends, we won't have any. In every relationship, we find balance or imbalance by the way we interact with another. It's like a dance we develop from the beginning when things are fresh and exciting. He is attentive, encouraging, and your biggest fan. He lets you make decisions on where you want to go because he wants to *make you happy.* You enjoy being able to show him all your favorite places, your favorite foods, and your favorite hobbies. He smiles and is a willing participant to everything about you but offers very little of himself saying he doesn't like to talk about himself, he really "doesn't care what we do" and doesn't have a favorite—anything. Eventually, you begin to feel frustrated that he won't take the lead on anything, and you begin to realize this dance is where you do all the leading. You make all the plans, do all the scheduling, and often pay for the night out. You develop uncomfortable feelings about taking on the leadership role but convince yourself that as long as he's willing and continues to smile, you will tolerate the discomfort. After a while, you get tired of leading and ask him to lead. He becomes angry and defensive, and you start to fight a lot. You don't understand why he is so resistant to taking the lead. He won't even pick a restaurant, won't participate in your favorite activities, or do any of the things he was willing to do in the beginning of the relationship. There appears to be a complete *flip* of his personality, and you become confused, frustrated, and discouraged. You have just realized that this person does not know how to lead or, if he knows how, will not take the lead by choice.

There are several reasons why he may resist leading. He could have experienced trauma as a child where he was not allowed to lead, he may have experienced failure or criticism when he attempted to lead, or he may simply be lazy and not interested in leading because whoever leads is responsible for the outcome (success or failure) and consequences.

Often, we hear our friend's stories and feel compassion but don't look beyond the pain to the person they have become. Some people overcome the challenges they faced as a child and go on to do great things. They may take their pain and turn it into purpose. They may take a job that is service oriented so they can help others whose life circumstances are similar to their own. They may create, develop, or inspire multitudes who hear their story and find hope. Sometimes, we can be sucked into their pain and miss how they are using it for selfish gain. They may excuse bad behaviors, bad choices, and negative consequences and blame their history for the outcomes. They may have criminal arrests, DUIs or made poor financial decisions. They may struggle every day of their life avoiding anything good because they see themselves as all bad. Either way, it is not your responsibility to rescue them. It is your responsibility to set healthy boundaries and limits to your relationship so you don't fall prey to their bad choices.

Girl power

Women have lost their power by giving it away. In the *old days*, young girls went to a school where they learned how to become valuable as a wife. The school was even called finishing school as it was the final stage to leaving childhood behind and finding a *suitable* husband. They were taught how to use their strengths and minimize their weaknesses. They learned how to cook, clean, and sew. They learned how to care for babies, and they learned about their sexuality and obligations as a wife to their husband. They were increasing their knowledge and learning how to be the best match for the man they desired to meet. They were also learning how to hook that man and lure him into marriage. They learned to be coy, flirtatious, and sweet. They were demure and played hard to get. They enticed the man to pursue them, and they only gave in to sexual temptations when they were wed. The marriages of old were lasting and families stayed together "until death."

Then came the sexual revolution, and women's liberation destroyed all that. The movement of the 1960s was driven by lust and a desire for sexual equality. It opened the door to destroying the family by tearing apart everything that defined gender roles. If a man could have sex out of wedlock, so could a woman. If a man could have multiple sexual partners, so could a woman. Women wanted what men had, and in order to control men, they stopped acting like the women of the past and started acting more like men. Women got jobs outside of the home and wanted their husbands to learn how to cook, clean, and take care of the children. Eventually, the concept of marriage was destroyed, and more single moms ended up raising their children alone unsupported by the men they rejected. More women are dying from stress-related heart issues, cancer, and are heavily medicated to address anxiety and depression than ever before. Yes, some women may be earning higher wages, work in corporate-level jobs, and may even run corporations, but at what cost? There are many more women living in poverty today than ever before. When women bought into the lie that becoming a man's equal meant power, we gave up the true power we had and ended up with something we never wanted in the first place. Women who want those high-paying jobs but must be available to their children are forced to take the lower-paying jobs that have more flexibility. They are overwhelmed, underappreciated, and overmedicated. They have fewer options, less money, less support, more stress, and less joy.

Women need to recognize the power they have in a relationship is not determined by their partner but by the personal standards she lives by. When women stop accepting the limitations others place on them, they will live limitlessly. When women stop allowing others to demean and minimize their worth, they will see they have value beyond jewels. When women stop listening to their friends and family tell them they have no destiny, they will search for the stars they are destined to reach. When women as a collective group stop giving sex away for free, men will respect women more. When women unite with a common goal to return to the family unit and stop having children by multiple partners out of wedlock, children will thrive. When we intentionally choose one partner who has the same desire for family, then families will stay together, and children will benefit from having both father and mother in the home. When women stand against the lies that led us down this path of single parenting and return to the standards that made us feel valued, honored, and respected, then we can again respect ourselves.

Performers and voyeurs

Sometimes when friends get together, they develop a relationship dance similar to the love dance. Someone is usually leading, and someone is often following. As friends, you can see this dance defined more by the way people watch and others perform. The role in the relationship is determined by the need for one person to be the *performer* and one to be the *voyeur*. Performer personalities are more outgoing, gregarious, inclusive, and social, inviting everyone into the relationship arena. They may be at their best when at parties and gatherings, large and small. They do most of the talking, laughing, and entertaining, and they thrive on the attention they receive from others. The performer needs someone else to perform for, so they attract voyeurs.

Here's an example of how the relationship dance looks between a voyeur (we'll call Ron) and a performer (we'll call Monica). The voyeur has no interest in performing or gaining the attention of others and is happy to just watch the show. It's like the performer is on a stage, and the voyeur is watching the relationship unfold, and they see themselves as playing a minor supporting role. They feel they are giving to the relationship simply by their presence. They give their attention, their approval, and their applause. They are at first so appreciative of the hard work Monica is giving them that they shower affections, attention, and gifts upon Monica. After a while, Ron gets tired of watching the same show and start looking for someone or something else to entertain them. They may return to the habits and hobbies they had prior to meeting Monica (gaming, pornography, gambling, etc.). This upsets Monica who has become aware they have lost their audience, and arguments erupt as Monica demands Ron's attention. Ron becomes defensive, angry, and resists by disconnecting completely. He sees his responsibility in this relationship as to be the happy observer, but he is no longer happy. Ron is now unhappy with the show and needs new stimulation, and Monica fears she will lose his attention altogether. Monica reacts to the disconnect by attempting to find new ways to entertain Ron and must compete with anything new that catches Ron's attention.

In the meantime, Ron enjoys the freedom to explore everything as his happiness is all that matters. Monica may complain that she cannot keep up with his insatiable desire for something new, and he remains unmotivated to change and feels harassed, criticized, and shamed into doing something he didn't sign up for. Ron blames Monica as he was and still is her audience, encourager, supporter, and approver, and he feels upset that Monica disapproves and does not give him credit for his effort.

The challenge for Monica is that she needs her Ron more than he needs her. He can leave the theatre and find another performer anytime, and she knows it. Monica, on the other hand, must start over finding someone who will want to watch their performance. Ron quits participating because the relationship is no longer fun. They quit helping with chores at home, raising the children, or participating in family functions. He is "there," but he isn't engaged. He becomes a liability to the relationship, another responsibility Monica must take care of, and it can become exhausting. Monica has no ability to change Ron, and all efforts to motivate him are futile. Ron *must* have a desire to change, or no change will happen.

There are usually two resolutions expressed by performers who come to counseling: the performer must always perform with no expectation of ever seeing the voyeur participate in their relationship, or they terminate the relationship looking for another person to dance with (and usually the pattern repeats because they are attracted to voyeurs). Often, the decision for Monica to move one way or the other isn't made for several months and even years as Ron may refuse to leave the relationship; they like getting everything their way, having all the control, and suffering no consequences. Monica can feel trapped as they concede that a disengaged Ron is better than no audience at all.

Change in the relationship is possible if Ron has a reason to change. He must first see that his unwillingness to participate is the problem, not his mate. Often, the fear of putting oneself out there is overwhelming because voyeurs mistakenly think they have to take the place of the performer in order to repair the relationship. Ron might enjoy being on stage occasionally and may even help now and again, but they do not feel it is their strength. The goal is not to make Ron a full-time performer but to give Monica "a break" occasionally. Ron can be more supportive and more of a team player if they know what specifically is expected of them. A good therapist can offer suggestions, books to read, and emotional support to help Ron understand a compromise is possible, and with only a few slight changes, the show can go on!

Foolish

The Reese's candy commercial unapologetically excuses selfishness by saying, "Sorry… Not sorry!" The actor explains he's going to eat his Halloween candy and not answer the door to the children seeking a trick or treat. This desire to please only self reflects a microcosm of society's lack of consideration and courtesy toward others. Why is it okay that everybody pursues their own wants even if it hurts others? Why do we have to flip everyone the bird, ignore their feelings, burn, bash, and destroy in order to feel valued, vindicated, and respected? And why has this become the acceptable norm for today? Why is a hate crime now excused as a "peaceful demonstration" depending on which side of the issue you stand? Why? Because there is no longer a standard for what is right, good, and just. When abuse happens in society, it's bound to affect relationships as conflict replaces compromise and abuse replaces love.

I found a plaque on a wall in a BBQ stand during a visit to Virginia. It was surrounded by photos of military personnel from all branches and eras in American history. The words written by Marcus Luttrell were framed in the center of the photos, "We were still confident. And we were never going to surrender. If it came down to it, we would fight to the death with our knives against their guns."

A man of conviction is a man unstoppable. Anyone surrounded by friends who would fight to the death alongside of them, for honorable reasons, is a group of people to be admired. People who will fight against tyranny, seeking justice, and to protect the lives of others is a beautiful thing. If you want to be surrounded by these types of people, you must go where they are, do what they do, and embrace the love they embrace. Passion and purpose alone do not make anyone honorable. Honor is knowing who you are and doing the right thing even when those around you are not.

Denial

One of the most discouraging things that a therapist must face is another person's denial and refusal to change. I think everyone who is trying to help someone else out of a difficult situation can feel discouraged. Some people may offer help by giving advice, money, or even by expressing a desire to walk in and pull them from that difficulty. Unfortunately, all too often, the one who claims he/she needs to be rescued is the one who goes right back into the unsafe situation over and over again. I saw this repeatedly with domestic-violence victims and addiction. Habitual denial has created an epidemic of victimization across the world. When people refuse to acknowledge the danger and would rather live in denial of it, they choose to be more comfortable with their abuser than uncomfortable alone. To break the cycle of abuse, you must create a new cycle of change. But it requires personal responsibility and acceptance of the fact that the change must start with you.

There is an old saying, "Misery loves company." It's not fun facing adversity and challenges alone. Some people would rather sit in their misery than make the effort to change. They say, "I'd rather be miserable with you than miserable without you." Sigmund Freud, the Father of Psychology, once said, "Most people do not really want freedom, because freedom involves responsibility, and most people are frightened of responsibility." It is the fear of responsibility that keeps people stuck, but what they truly are afraid of is the unknown. They don't know how much effort it will take to change, what consequences might result from it, or if change is even possible for them. And what if they do change? Who will they become? But they are not happy with the person they are either because they are not living as their authentic self. Author Will Witt states it this way, "How much of myself am I willing to sacrifice to appease other people until I am no longer the person, I thought I was?" When we forfeit ourselves for the sake of another's happiness, we lose our true identity.

Codependency further plays an evil trick on people by causing them to loose themselves in a pattern of unhealthy relationships. People who have been raised in an unhealthy family, as an adult, will seek out other unhealthy people because that feels "normal." The thought of doing something that does not feel familiar or pushes them out of their comfort zone is scarier than the situation in which they find themselves. There is a false sense that somehow, they think they can control this situation, but they may not be able to control the unknown situation. Until they are willing to be stretched, they will remain stuck.

Until someone is willing to get stretched a little, they have no perspective that anything could be different. The amazing thing about people who are eager to take the risk of change is, they are the ones who change most dramatically. It's how a new pair of boots feel uncomfortable until they get broken in and become your favorite footwear. People can love the new person they are becoming so much that the thought of change is no longer scary, and they begin to seek out change. They are successful because they overcame their fear of the unknown and learned to fly. They soar above their circumstances and have gained a new perspective that allows them to see more clearly. They allowed a new possibility to take flight, and they are better for it.

> *A man who hurts people tempts his neighbor*
> *to do the same, and leads him in a way that is not*
> *good.* (Proverbs 16:29 NIV)

CHAPTER 9

Intentional Communication

Where there is strife, there is pride, but wisdom
is found in those who take advice.
—Proverbs 13:10 (NIV)

Communication breakdown is the number one reason couples come to therapy. They may have different personality styles, communication styles, or differing objectives and goals in mind when they are trying to communicate. They may need to speak while they think about what they want to say, and they may only want the bottom line and not all the fluff that accompanies the communication. They may be solution focused, or they may be connection focused. Communication styles can create conflict, and with someone who has trauma, communication can be very complicated. I'd like to provide an approach to creating an environment to communicate with intent.

Imagine, we all have two minds: one logical and the other emotional. When one is speaking logically, they are speaking with facts and figures, and they have much content to offer to support their position. When someone is speaking from their emotional "heart," they are sharing their pains, fears, and worries. Those feelings often are more about intuition and projections based on fear. They usually don't have facts to support them, and feelings seldom change even when presented facts to the contrary. Have you ever changed how you feel simply because someone said, "You shouldn't feel that way"? We now are living in a world where communication is no longer breaking down; it is broken. We used to avoid difficult conversations like religion, sex, and politics, but all that has changed to where all we seem to talk about are the many changes and challenges of all three. Unfortunately, forced communication with challenging content can create more pain than serve a real purpose.

Healthy communication can be restored if the people involved are willing to take the time to learn and practice some simple steps to conflict resolution. It takes two to have a fight, and it takes two willing participants to resolve the conflict. Sometimes, a professional mediator (therapist) can help because they are trained to help where friends and family members are not and can get wrapped up in the emotion because they can't distance themselves sufficiently.

I suggest to my clients that they must first set up the preconversation safety zone. Be intentional. This means setting a time, place, and environment where they will not be distracted in the middle of the conversation. This conversation does not take place on *date night* or just before you go to bed. Depending on the topic and how many times it has been bought up without resolution, they might need to get a hotel room away from the children or send them on an overnighter to their grandparent's house.

Once the place and time has been set, the environment must be conducive to uninterrupted focus. Don't talk over dinner at a crowded restaurant. Eat first. Make sure you are rested. Don't start the conversation late in the evening. Don't start preempting the conversation on the drive to the destination. Find a place that is peaceful, quiet, and comfortable. Face each other and hold hands. Determine who will start the conversation and who will be first to listen.

When the speaking begins, listener, don't interrupt. Setting a timer works well if one person talks too long, goes off course, or is easily distracted. Setting a timer for 3–5 minutes helps also if one person has ADHD or OCD and can't stay focused for long periods of time. You might need to take a huge topic and break it into bite-size topics. As they say, "You can eat an elephant one bite at a time."

Don't expect the listener to consume every problem you have all at once. Don't bring a laundry list of problems. Pick *one* issue to discuss and stay on topic.

It's also beneficial to write down what it is you want to say. Write it with a goal in mind and a date when you would like the task, situation, or resolution to be completed. If it's an unfinished task that is the problem, write what it would take to get it done, costs involved, and the desired date of completion. If the subject is regarding a situation, how does it get resolved? Don't just bring someone your problem and then ask them to solve it for you. It's your problem, and it's unfair to dump it on someone else. If you are only asking permission to resolve the problem and seek their support, seek understanding first before you enlist their help.

If your desire is a change in your partner, realize that change must be their choice. You can point out the behavior or pattern and the impact of their behavior has on you, the kids, finances, etcetera, but ultimately, you are only providing them your perspective of the problem. Your goal is to provide insight, information, and support for the choice you hope they will make. You can set boundaries on how long you will tolerate the problematic behavior, advise them of potential consequences if they don't change, but you cannot demand that they change. Enter the conversation with hope, a desire for healing, and with both minds engaged.

Be responsible for your own two minds: logical and emotional. Remember, logic does not communicate with emotion, and you must both be in the same mindset in order to communicate well.

Lastly, realize that communication is talking *with* someone else, not *at* them. Lecturing without the other's permission is not communication. Telling someone your complaint and walking out of the room is not communication. Refusing to listen to their side unless they agree with you is not communication. When two people can be patient, kind, caring, and listen with the intention to learn, communication can be amazing.

Guilt

Recently, I heard someone say, "Peace only happens when everyone stops to reload." In many relationships where false guilt is common, this saying could feel very true. Have you ever been accused of something that's not true? Have you ever told someone, "How can you say that? You don't even know me." Have you felt that someone you married, had children with, or who has known you for years still doesn't really know you? They may know a portion of your history and the challenges you've had to overcome. They may know the life you've led, the path you took, and even the choices you made that resulted in where you are today. But no one can really know us as well as we know ourselves—our character, our truth.

Unrealistic expectations have their foundations rooted in our family of origin. Parents and siblings often believe we should *know* things about them because we grew up around them. We should *know* what is hurtful to them, what triggers them, and what makes them want to fight or push back. Notice I said these are "unrealistic expectations" because no one can really meet all your expectations. Even when we look at ourselves, we can have unrealistic expectations because knowing doesn't always translate into doing. We don't do for ourselves the good things that we know we should. We eat the wrong things, drink the wrong drinks, say the wrong words, and do the wrong actions. So knowing who we are doesn't necessarily mean doing what's best for us. If we can't get ourselves to behave, how can we have an expectation that others would behave better than we do ourselves? When we give ourselves grace and deny it to others, we can accuse others of being uncaring, insensitive to our feelings, and even destroy, harm, and murder them all because of unmet expectations that demand agreement and compliance. This is manipulative, and it is abusive.

False guilt makes us wonder what we did wrong. We replay the situation, the accusations, and question our memory as if we got the story wrong. When the accusation holds more power than the truth, it can be mind-blowing. We can apologize and take responsibility for the lie even knowing it's not true but feeling like it's the only way to stop the painful attack on our character. After a while, we begin to believe that the accusations are true and fall into shame-filled despair. This is what it feels like to be bullied.

The way we overcome this type of abuse is to not listen to the lies and don't accept them as your responsibility. When someone brings you a lie, you can try to persuade them to the truth. But when others insist their perspective (even if it's a lie) is truth, all you can do is walk away. This is a battle you won't win, and you will be the one left emotionally bloodied and beaten up. A client shared that he looks at handling this form of confrontation by comparing his response to finishing a chapter in a book. "If I try to reread it, it's going to be the same—the same words, the same story, the same experience. Nothing changes. I need to close that chapter and move on."

Trust

So how can we ever trust anyone after we've been so deeply hurt? Can we ever completely trust anyone? It seems to be getting harder and harder to trust anyone but ourselves. Even that seems to be a partial truth as we can be telling ourselves lies and living deceived. I encourage people to be always truth seekers first, to challenge why there is distraction and avoidance to honesty. Why is deflection, redirection, and projection the result of direct questions? When someone asks point-blank, "Are you having an affair?" and the answer is to blame, challenge, and avoid, you have your answer. If they confess their "mistake" and ask for forgiveness, don't forgive too soon. Really? Yes. If you forgive without setting consequences and conditions for earning your trust again, you will only resent and suspect them of future affairs. This applies to all forms of deception.

Consequences

When someone has deceived another, they have shown themselves to be untrustworthy. In other words, you can't trust them. So in order to forgive and move on, you must rebuild that trust.

Forgiveness does not alone create trust. Trust is built by repeatedly doing things that build trust and developing a pattern of behavior consistent with the things that are said. Actions speak louder than words, and follow-through, commitment, and keeping your word are the actions that build trust. Expectations and conditions that follow consequences are not set by the offender but by the one who was offended. Here are a few examples of consequences and conditions:

> You broke my heart when you lied to me. I can't trust you anymore. I want you to sleep in the guest room until you show me I can trust you again (consequence). I want you to put a block on your phone, the laptop, and tablet that will keep out the porn. I also want you to go with me to therapy (condition).

> When you grabbed me last night during a drinking rage, you hurt me. I can't trust you to be safe anymore and want you to move out (consequence). If you want to come back home, you must go into treatment for your addiction, get a sponsor in AA, and go to therapy with me so we can rebuild the trust (condition).

When the other is willing to accept the consequences and meet your conditions, you can rebuild trust. When they refuse, diffuse, and minimize their actions, you will never be able to trust them again. You will always wonder, doubt, and feel the consequences for their choices that leave you only one option, to accept the lie and deny the truth. Eventually, it won't be deception anymore because you know the truth and choose to tolerate the behavior. Eventually, you will realize that choosing to stay in the relationship means you give up hope, happiness, and love. The black swan unexpected event has come to roost, and you've allowed it to stay.

Many couples will live together miserably rather than be miserable alone. Don't be one of those miserable people who lock themselves up in a prison of their own making so they can blame another for their pain. Unlock the door and set yourself free. No one is keeping you there except your choices. Change your choice to walking in truth, living in understanding, and embrace the life you deserve. It's so much better to chase the black swan from your life and set yourself free.

Twisted

One of the most twisty roads in the world is the Trollstigen in Rauma, Norway. Drivers wind back and forth, accelerating in the straightaways and decelerating as they approach the sharp curves. It is guaranteed to be a wild ride for anyone who ventures there. Sometimes, when we communicate our thoughts, we can talk in pathways that lead us up twisty roads toward unseen mountaintops. We speed up and slow down, emphasize the challenges, and talk about how painful it is to constantly be stepping on the breaks when what we really want is a straightaway to speed us to the final destination.

Some people drive communication in this type of twisting and turning because they are verbal thinkers who need to hear themselves speak to further gain insight for the discussion. When the speaker (driver) is sharing their experiences, their concerns, their hurts, their perspectives, and their solutions, the listener (passenger) can become impatient with the twists and turns and will interrupt. These distractions may cause conflict because the speaker who is trying to drive up the twisting road must detour to answer a question that is not a part of the planned journey. It's like racing up the hill and getting a flat. The curse words that follow are the reaction to the interruption, not necessarily to what is being said. This results in the listener being put off, placated, or ignored as the driver keeps focused as they press forward to their final destination, which is their concluding thought (the point they are trying to make). The listener must go along for the ride, patiently not interrupting, and is required to listen to every twist and turn, speed up and slow down, until the final thought has been processed to its final conclusion. *That* is the point they are trying to make. *That* is what the speaker wants you to hear. Unfortunately, the passengers have fallen asleep halfway up the road or are more concerned about their own thoughts and feelings of hurt, defensiveness, and disagreements as they impatiently wait for the journey to end. This mismatched communication repeated over time results in one person constantly feeling misunderstood and the other feeling unheard.

When I work with people who are verbal processors, I show them how to write their questions, concerns, and suggestions on a piece of paper to present to their listener. They can process out loud as they write, contemplate, and ponder these thoughts away from the person they are trying to speak with. Once they have figured out what the *point* is, they offer the condensed version of their communication for discussion. When the passenger knows the journey will be shorter, they will be more willing to patiently listen and may engage more in conversation. Often, I share with my clients a concept for how they are holding their partner accountable for a thought they never had. Often, I hear the accusation that one person has against the other for how they think the other person is feeling, thinking, or wanting with no evidence that the other person is feeling, thinking, or wanting anything of the sort. When this happens, we falsely accuse others of crimes (thoughts and actions) and convict them based on our feelings and not on the facts.

> *An understanding mind gets much learning,*
> *and the ear of the wise listens for much learning.*
> (Proverbs 18:15 NIV)

CHAPTER 10

Intentional Finances

Let no debt remain outstanding,
except the continuing debt to love one another,
for whoever loves others has fulfilled the law.
—Romans 13:8 (NIV)

The second reason why people argue is disagreement over their finances. Therefore, you must handle your finances wisely and intentionally.

The world is moving at the speed of light, and many like me don't like it. Recently, I went to get a new bank card and was told to download the bank's app. I told the teller I didn't want an app on my phone (I miss the days when a phone was only a phone), and the woman said, "It's the way we communicate with our customers now." She tried to tell me all the benefits of banking on my phone, and I told her I like the feel of money in my hand, I like paper statements, I like writing checks, and I like getting help from the walk-up teller. I feel pressured to take unwanted risks and take chances that technology will fail, and I'll not have access to my finances. Experience has shown me that cyberattacks allow thieves to steal personal information are becoming more and more common with breaches at hospitals, stores, and even our government. How can the bank protect my money from cyber theft? I now see why people in the old days stuffed their hard-earned money in the mattresses.

Financial methods of the past allowed people to have tangible assets they could see and feel. You knew if you had money in the bank, you could usually withdraw it during business hours minus weekends and holidays. Then the ATM machine made it more accessible. I found it odd that they replaced the teller with the ATM, and we had to pay a fee for using the machine, but I still could access a live human being if I had a question. As phone banking apps, electronic bill pay, and a cashless society become more common, customer service that is already rapidly disappearing will be altogether gone. Communist China already has begun to implement a cashless society where every transaction is processed through a government-issued phone that deposits their earnings, records all spending, and controls their people's ability to spend. The citizens are excited about the simplicity and convenience of not having to worry about carrying identification, loosing credit or debit cards, or having to make exact change. They use the app on the phone, and facial recognition confirms the phone is theirs. It may be nice not to have to carry a wallet or purse when everything is on your phone, but I'm skeptical about who is in control of my money. Consider, if you do something that is not approved or fail to follow the rules, will the government (bank) shut off your phone? Also, when you have no phone, you cannot earn a living, and you cannot borrow money from a friend to buy food. Ultimately, does no phone mean no identity, and you just disappear? I would rather be inconvenienced and retain control of my money. Unfortunately, I feel this is another cliff we are going to blindly walk off and won't know the ramifications until it is too late. It is important to remember that when it comes to money, he who has the money has the power. There's more cryptic to cryptocurrency than the eye can see.

I was looking up truisms online to see what common folks of the past said about money. An online dictionary states *truism* is a "phrase or sentence that sounds meaningful and profound on the surface but does not impart any new information or ideas. Generally, a truism is self-evident or obvious." They are statements rooted in accumulated experience proven over time which are accepted as fact. Here are a few:

- Money is power, freedom, a cushion, the root of all evil, the sum of blessings. It doesn't matter about money—having it, not having it—or having clothes or not having them. You're still left alone with yourself in the end. The safe way to double your money is to fold it over once and put it in your pocket.
- "Money has never made man happy, nor will it. There is nothing in its nature to produce happiness. The more of it one has, the more one wants" (Benjamin Franklin).
- "Too many people spend money they haven't earned, to buy things they don't want, to impress people that they don't like" (Will Rogers).

Recently, it seems we have lost many truisms about wealth and equity, and they are being replaced by new self-evident statements which have no basis in truth but are being presented as fact. Here are some truths about recent misrepresentations:

- Shame for one race does not elevate pride in another.
- Self-esteem is not improved from getting a trophy you didn't earn.
- Wealth is not gained by removing another's ability to earn.
- Working hard to succeed does not make you privileged, and lacking motivation does not make you underprivileged.

Equality cannot be achieved at the level of excellence while settling for the lowest common denominator.

> *The absence of evidence is not evidence of absence.* (Carl Sagan)

Complacency

Procrastination is at epidemic proportions across our nation. We will put off everything; even living our lives has been put on hold during the 2020 pandemic. All that *wait and see* has us stuck in the weeds, and it's harder and harder to step out and step up and fulfill our responsibilities. As long as someone else is doing the work, as we don't have to perform, we don't have to try. If we don't try, we won't fail. If we don't fail, doesn't that make us successful? Well, if your goal is to only survive on the gifts of others, then I guess you have been successful. But when others don't provide the means for you to be more profitable, more accomplished, or more successful because you are not adding anything additional to what they provide, then you are stuck only getting what others will give. In other words, when you chose to live in mediocrity, you will live in mediocrity. When you chose to improve your lifestyle, you must choose to put forward the effort necessary to better your life.

When the pandemic of 2020–2021 was in full force, many sat on the couch playing video games or watching the looping news reports. Fewer people went to work. Even fewer people took the time to expand on their knowledge, read books, and study the political and economic climate. Business owners took advantage of the slow-down to prepare for the ramp-up. That last group will be the ones who make billions of dollars post pandemic. Those who sat waiting to be told what to do were so far behind the curve they will never catch up, and for many, the effects will be devastating. The lessons learned were harsh. The ramifications for inactivity are still felt today as the consequences for procrastination linger.

So how do you avoid another financial crisis? Get off the couch and go get a job. Right now, competition is low as the blue-collar worker has become complacent and comfortable in their lack of pro-vision. Many have resolved to live in mediocrity and lack rather than work to succeed. When they find they have run out of resources, when the landlords sell their home out from under them, when they have no food to feed their babies, they may want to go to work but may find there are no jobs available. That's why the time to act is *now*. Don't put it off another moment, waiting until the unemployment checks run out. It could be too late. Return to work, prove your value to your employer, and you might find yourself climbing the ladder to pay raises and promotions that no one else is competing for. And continue to increase your value. Read, learn, and teach others to do the same. The perpetual learner is always going to be the most successful (and valuable) person in the room because, as I tell my clients, friends, family, and colleagues, "When you change, everything will change."

Trapped

People across America are feeling the financial pinch. The cost of food, gas, and health care are skyrocketing, and there are fewer and fewer service providers available to meet the needs of the masses. I believe it's going to get much worse before it gets better. At the time of this writing, Christmas gifts were unavailable due to looting (criminals were able to steal without fear of consequences), the trucking industry was impacted by new government regulations, COVID mandates forced workers out of jobs, and international trade was halted when the supply chain was broken. Thousands of shipping cargo boxes were left at sea, and fear of supply shortages had people hoarding food and water and, dare I say, toilet paper, for a second time since the pandemic.

Inflation is the next wave that will hit Americans, and many financial experts are saying uncontrolled government spending will further cause harm to the average citizen who is still reeling from the effects of COVID shutdowns and vaccine mandates.

So what can individuals and families do when the incomes don't go up but the expenses do? Cut back. They cut back on dining out, going to the movies, and traveling to friends and family members who live beyond their city borders. They isolate, get depressed, and feel discouraged. Everywhere we look, there is a shrinking ability to return to what was normal pre-COVID. Families and friends are angry at all the changes and the solutions that cause more harm than offer help.

Prepare

There is a saying, "Prepare for the worst and hope for the best." When I speak of being intentional with your financial security, I am talking about every aspect of life that involves money. This means everything from your food, housing, clothing, and other basics of survival that once were in abundance and of little concern. For decades Americans have been blessed to be able to go to a store and purchase food and few of us have faced starvation. As more and more people enter our country, our storehouses are being emptied, and people are living and dying on our streets. The things we took for granted are now in short supply, and there is a fight for America's limited resources.

When we have no plan for our money, we are forced to react to the lack of it. Are you planning how much money you will spend before you spend it? Do you have a budget that shows you exactly where your money is going, or do you just spend until it's gone? Do you hope and pray you'll be able to replace it with the next paycheck, loan, or government check? What is your plan if you lose your job, can't get a loan, and those replacement funds don't arrive? If you have no plan, by default, your plan is to fail.

This year, creating a strategic plan for purchases that is realistic to the size of your budget requires you to be intentional with your finances. When you put numbers on a paper, you can see the math and if your plan is working or not. When you make $1,000 a week and spend $1,025, you can see you are over your budget at a glance. When you don't do the math, you will never know if your budget is balanced, and you'll be guessing your way further into debt.

Credit cards can be useful when you know how to pay them off every month. Some people can make purchases on their cards and receive credits for travel or cash refunds, but it takes discipline and commitment to pay off the cards with the money you've earned for that purpose. Most people are not disciplined and will find themselves unable to pay for the goods and services they charged because they also spent the money meant to pay for them. Financial planner Dave Ramsey (Ramsey.com) suggests using envelopes with cash to pay for all purchases. He says that when you have an envelope with money in it, you'll "feel it" when you spend the dollars. You'll also know when you've spent your limit because the envelope will be empty. With debit and credit cards, it's easy to lose track of how much you've spent, and you don't feel the pain until your next statement when see your bank account is empty, and your rent check bounces. Then the late fees begin to pile up. All this stress could have been avoided with a little preplanning.

One thing I learned to do many years ago was to purchase my Christmas presents all year long. I would start at the after-Christmas sales and would finish up my list with the "back to school" sales. I also would buy one $25 gift card a month that gave me a handful of options for friends, my boss, and coworkers who I forgot to buy a gift for. This strategy helped me stay calm when everyone else was frantically shopping on Christmas Eve. If you'd like to learn more strategies on healthy spending, check out this podcast: *The Fine Print with George Kamel* (thefineprint@ramseysolutions.com). Also, you can download a free budgeting app at EveryDollar.com. Decide to take time at Christmas to focus on love. It is free to give and receive, and the memories are going to last long after the toys are broken, lost, or forgotten.

Steps

Step one to being financially intentional is to know where you currently stand financially. Where is your money locked up? If you live paycheck to paycheck, this is a problem because you have nothing in reserve. If you spend everything *left over*, then you need to stop excessive spending. If you spend more than you make and supplement your income with credit cards, you are living on the edge of financial ruin. Even if you have a small savings account, will it be enough to live on if you lose your ability to earn? The average working individual has only enough resources in their bank account to sustain them thirty days. If you are relying on government assistance and food stamps, your chances of lasting that long are greatly diminished if the government assistance stops. Take a hard look at your current financial situation, and when you pick yourself up off the floor, do step two.

Step two to being financially intentional is to have a plan. Without a plan of how to change your circumstances, you will not take necessary action to correct and stop the financial bleeding. When you know what is broken, it's much easier to fix. When you put a Band-Aid over a hemorrhaging problem, you may slow the bleeding, but you eventually will suffer the consequences. Avoidance has become the solution of choice, but you need a plan for when that choice is no longer available to you.

Step three is to create a budget. If you have never created a budget, it's very simple and not as complicated as people would have you think. These are the simple steps that any sixth grader can do:

1. Write down your total household income. If you are the sole income earner, it's the total of *take-home* pay that you receive. This can be a government check or wages you earn from a job.

2. Make a list of *everything* you spend your money on. These are expenses. Once you have itemized your bills, food, clothing, housing, utilities, insurance (car, home, medical), gas, school, credit card debt, and year-end taxes, you'll soon begin to see why you don't have much left over at the end of the month. Just seeing how much money is flowing out of your bank account is enough to drive the average individual into a state of depression.

3. The bottom line—this is where you subtract the expenses from the income to get an idea if you are living in perpetual debt (compounding monthly) or if you have anything left over (savings).

4. Balance the books. This is where you are going to make changes that will give you hope over your current financial situation. This is where you need to trim the fat. Identify areas that are not necessary. If you are wasting money on clothes that only pile up in the closet, if you throw out more food than you eat, if you spend more money on fast

food than you do eating at home, if your entertainment category is bulging, if you are wasting money on booze and cigarettes, if your internet bill is huge because of the gaming and binge watching, these are places where money can be saved. Fun and excitement are no longer your priority. Financial freedom and peace of mind are the goals you should pursue.

5. Live within your means. Once you have control over your spending and have a clear idea of how to save financial resources, begin focusing on other areas of your life that need to be downsized. Clean out the excess and live within your financial but also spatial confines of your life. If you have excess *stuff*, get rid of it, sell it, or donate it to a charity.

Step four is to create a savings-and-investment strategy. When the bills are paid, you have a six-month emergency fund, and you are debt free. You'll have more money at the end of the month, and those dollars need to have a job. They need to be wisely invested, and finding a financial planner to help you determine the best method is great, but remember, there are more ways to invest than in just the stock market. Timing is everything, and your goal is to buy *low* and sell *high*. Real estate, gold, and silver are also options. Angel investing, business development, and many other investment options are available but seldom discussed. Planning for this stage of your life is so you will have a nest egg for retirement, travel, and to splurge on your grandchildren.

Step five happens naturally when you are debt free, live within your means, and have your priorities right. You'll be able to focus on other things in your life that bring you joy. Get rid of the clutter, get rid of the burdens, and live intentional in all aspects of your life. As you lessen financial debt and downsize the spatial excess, you'll notice you feel lighter and less anxious and depressed overall.

Money is a blessing if it is handled wisely and spending is controlled. It can be a blessing you can hand down to your children. Being intentional with your finances takes time, patience, and a willingness to learn. It helps to work hard during the early years of your life so you won't have to work hard or have regrets *the rest of your life.*

> *For the love of money is a root of all kinds of evil. Some people, eager for money, have wandered from the faith and pierced themselves with many griefs.* (1 Timothy 6:10 NIV)

CHAPTER 11

Intentional Parenting

*Whoever is patient has great understanding, but
one who is quick-tempered displays folly.*
—Proverbs 14:29 (NIV)

Raising children requires intentionality. There are only 168 hours in a week in which to accomplish life. For the average parent with minor children, every one of those precious hours is divided into the caring of their children, their home, their marriage, and their faith. Not much is left over for themselves.

One of the most enjoyable benefits of my being a therapist is to work with young parents who are eager to improve their parenting skills. What I have found is a common problem with children coming to therapy: There is a lack of training occurring in the home. Parents are not instilling in their children the tools necessary to live full, meaningful, and successful lives. They may love "on" their children and smother them with kisses and hugs, but what about the real tools they will need to make it through every day of their adult lives? Let me give you just three examples of the most common trainings that are not occurring before the child leaves the home:

- *Diet.* Most moms are also working moms as the number of single-parent homes increase. This doesn't leave much time for teaching their children how to cook. So children become adults who spend way too much money on fast food or expensive restaurants. Oh, and forget about even making a grocery list or doing meal planning. They will suffer the consequences of not learning what is a healthy diet as they age and begin to have health issues related to a poor diet.

- *Money.* Few parents are teaching their teenagers how to budget their money. What's worse is they are not teaching them how to earn money. Teenagers are not getting jobs now as the availability of entry-level employment is being taken by uneducated adults. Parents tell their teens to go to college (where they incur huge debt they cannot pay) because they don't know what else to do. With no income and no idea how to earn it, these teens turn into twenty- to thirty-year-olds living at home with their parents with no momentum for personal growth.

- *Faith.* When parents unknowingly relinquished their parental rights to school districts, doctors, and their children's mentors (whoever they may be), they lost the power to influence their children toward any standard of *right and wrong.* Therefore, children are determining for themselves what is right (anything that feels good to them) and wrong (anything that does not feel good to me). This leaves everything up to personal interpretation, and any standard (legal, civil, cultural, family) cannot be imposed and does not apply. Faith and God become irrelevant.

Self-esteem

Teaching your little ones that they are special and unique and a blessing from God is foundational to their self-esteem. When we know who we are in the eyes of those who love us, our self learns to respect ourselves as well as respect others. Self-respect determines the quality of life we will live, and our relationships will be defined by what we will tolerate.

Self-doubt is easy to accept. When we don't have confidence in what is true, we can be swayed to believe a lie. Parents, not teachers, are responsible for teaching their children truth. When your children ask you for counsel, give it. When they want to know your thoughts, share them. When they are confused, give them clarity. Character is developed and improved not because of the challenges in our life but despite them. We are all going to experience difficulty no matter what our differences are. Identity opposition is when we choose to not fit in the box others made for us. Cancel culture rejects those individuals who do not conform to the lies pressed upon them and who ultimately reject the premise that everyone needs to be the same in order to be unique.

Individuality

I believe that we can conform in certain aspects of life without losing our individuality. We can conform to the laws of the land, to following the rules of the road, and to living a life that blesses others as we receive blessings ourselves. I believe we must evaluate each circumstance for truthfulness, and to conform to lies in order to belong is ill-advised. When you find yourself agreeing with the majority, it's time to question your own judgment. When you see your children conforming without understanding, it's time to step in and teach them reasons to conform or to reject. When people begin to think for themselves, everyone wins. When we blindly conform, we, like sheep, can be led over a cliff we can't see.

You can't influence everyone, but you can influence one.

Adulting

When these twentysomething adults come to me complaining that their parents won't treat them like adults, I ask them how they are showing their parents they *are* adults. This gets me a sideways tilt of the head as they inquire, "What do you mean?"

I show them how they are still acting like a child. "Who pays for your housing? Who pays for your food? Who pays for your clothes? Who does your laundry? Who prepares your meals? Who pays for the gas in your car, and who pays for your schooling?"

I usually get a scowl and "now you sound like my parents" response

I tell them, "Just because you turned eighteen years old does not make you an adult."

We then begin the journey of understanding what it means to be a productive, independent, and successful adult. This journey is actually fun for them as they learn how to create a budget, fill out a résumé, apply for a job, and start on the pathway of independence. I show them that as they gain speed being an adult, they should take these life lessons (skills) and pass them purposefully onto their children. So, parents, I challenge you to love, teach, mentor, and preach God's love to your children even after they've become adults. They will be better for it, and I'll have fewer young adults in therapy seeking the counsel they could receive at home.

> *The Godly walk with integrity; blessed are their children who follow them.* (Proverbs 20:7 NIV)

Moral safety

While walking one day, I saw a sign affixed to the wall of a fire station that had on it a picture of a baby, and the words below said, "Safe Surrender Site." It made me think of the conflict that is going on between schools and parents and how this sign could apply to schools as well…or maybe not.

Children are both a blessing and a challenge. It's best to raise them with intentional parenting skills. Unfortunately, intentionality requires knowledge of what is happening in your children's lives and who the people are that are influencing them.

At what age should you begin to teach your children morality? Morality, or what is the measurement for what is moral, was established way before you were born, what your parents and their parents and prior generations passed down as concepts of morality, and those standards became their moral standing. When you accepted or rejected their moral standards, you created your own moral standard for what is right, wrong, or tolerable. When you live your life according to a personal standard of your making or no moral standard at all, there is no standard for what is moral you can teach your children. Your actions and words become the rules for what is moral, and your children learn not by what you teach them but by what they experience.

Often, the only moral guideposts for what is considered correct behavior can be found rooted in selfishness. When you determine for yourself what is morally correct, you can be both judge and jury, prosecutor and defender of your behaviors. You may judge yourself after you have committed the crimes (conviction), or you may release yourself for crimes against others not yet committed (grace). When you make the rules, you can also determine any consequences for injustices and who should pay. When your children see you committing offenses, then you judge them for their own; you are teaching them there is no justice at all. When your opinion is the truth, compliance is all that matters. Have you ever heard a child ask their parent why? The parent can teach the reason or demand obedience, "Because I said so. That's why!"

From the beginning of time, morality has been established by families who make up society. Even God failed as a parent when Adam and Eve broke his rules. Adam and Eve were cast out of the garden of Eden, and when their children were born, the moral consequences for their parents' break from morality (the original sin) resulted in the murder of one of their children by his sibling. I'm sure it was not the intention of Adam and Eve to raise children who would resort to such extremes, but their children did not learn morality from God (as Adam and Eve did) but from their parents. Morality continued down the slippery slope of selfishness until God couldn't take it anymore and sent a flood to destroy the world for a do-over with only one righteous family surviving. But even that attempt to reintroduce morality failed. Jesus was God's last attempt to establish a standard for morality, and the Bible is the written standard from God.

When a family uses the Bible to establish their moral foundation, they can always return to the written Word for guidance. Second Timothy 3:16–17 explains how we are to use the Bible to establish a foundation for what is moral in our personal life, our family, our relationships, friendships, to establish our work ethic, as well as how to function as a healthy member of society,

> *All Scripture is God-breathed and is useful for teaching, rebuking, correcting and training in righteousness, so that the servant of God may be thoroughly equipped for every good work.* (2 Timothy 3:16–17 NIV)

Moral parenting takes hard work because without consistency, it falls apart. You must live according to the principles you want to teach your children. I remember growing up and hearing, "Do as I say, not as I do," which was the standard of parents who grew up in the 1960s revolution. The hippy culture burned through America and the world, giving rise to immoral behaviors that were normalized, and over the years, we've come to embrace these immoral practices as our "right." The desensitization of what is immoral has brought only ruin to the family unit, confusion to our children, and displeasure with everyone and anything that does not make us happy. Because we only measure our lives through our experiences, we can blame others for how our experiences make us feel. I must look outside of myself for reasons for my unhappiness because I'm living according to their standards. If I believe the color of my skin determines my ability to succeed, then it must be racism that limits me. If I believe my gender limits my success, then I need to have ways to change my gender to succeed. If I believe marriage limits my ability to find happiness in a relationship, then divorce must be the way to succeed. If children are the reason for limiting me, abortion must be the solution. If the cause for my unhappiness can be blamed on another, then the way to eliminate my unhappiness is through avoidance, confrontation, and hate. The way to find happiness is not found through blaming others. To overcome obstacles in your life, you must be willing to take personal responsibility for the choices you make.

Recent attacks on parents' rights are the result of newly exposed legislation and school curriculum that continues to undermine the authority of parents. Recently, a law was passed that gives eleven-year-olds the right to undergo gender reassignment without the knowledge of their parents. Schools have been given authority over children by our governments, and parents' rights are being removed if not freely given away. I'm hearing more and more concern from parents who are being told they do not have the right to know any medical information about their minor children and are being denied access to even be present when doctors examine their children. It's true there are new HIPPA revisions, and parents need to stay current on those changes and how their rights are being affected. More and more laws are being passed that are removing the parent's right to know, right to deny, and right to inquire. The more rules and regulations that empower others means the less power and control parents have.

The world will ask you who you are, and if
you don't know, the world will tell you. (Carl Jung)

Having said that, there is hope for parents and their children. The younger your children are, the better the chances that you'll be able to regain or maintain influence over them. Parents who have lost the ability to influence their teenagers have become discouraged and fearful as they watch them isolate and spiral into depression. Recovery is possible, but it will need intentional parenting skills and focus to turn the tide. Remember always, no one will love, guide, and care for your child as well as you should, could, or do.

Directions please

Are you a parent who is trying to figure out how to be a "good" parent, even while you feel you are failing yourself, your children, and your spouse? I hope to encourage you today... We all feel lost as parents. The road is not clearly marked, and often, we learn too late that we were speeding down the wrong road entirely. Sometimes, we must turn around and go back in order to get on the right road. Isn't it funny that men make fun of women's driving, and women make fun of men who refuse to ask for directions? Maybe Moses (of the Bible) wouldn't have wondered in the desert forty years if he only would have asked for directions.

Often, we focus on the wrong things. We can receive a large bag of golden blessings and still complain at the weight of it. When someone finally pushes you to a place of discontent so big you must change, instead of resentment toward them, say, "Thank you for forcing a situation upon me that offered me a chance to grow." This is a blessing in disguise. Change is hard, but change must happen before opportunity to improve can occur.

You are not starting over when you take a step back. It is a move based on strategy. It's not a retreat. You are regrouping and preparing to implement a new strategy that will take you in a different direction. It is not failure; it is skill. It is not something to fear. It takes courage and insight to change direction. When you accept that sometimes moving forward requires us to change direction, even the direction of stepping back, we can influence others to adjust in their actions as well. Our insecurities can be passed down to our children who also are trying to maneuver through life. Likewise, our courage can be handed down when others see how we address challenges, not with fear but in faith and that faith put into action.

When it seems too simple, it isn't. When it seems too hard, it isn't.

Everyone needs opportunity. Unfortunately, many parents reject opportunity when it comes along. Their own fear prevents their children from attempting to succeed by not opening the door when opportunity knocks. Children need to be allowed to enter into opportunity as if walking through that door. There is a saying, "Opportunity only knocks once," and you can miss it if you don't jump on it. Not only should parents allow their children to grow and experience, but they also need to encourage it. They need to open the door and walk *with* their children through the door, being supportive of the effort and courage it takes to reach for the unknown. Who knows what the outcome will be to attempting to gain success? If you never try, you know the outcome is failure. But if you try and don't succeed, try, try, again. Failure only happens when you quit, and when quitting is not an option, the sky is the limit.

When my daughter was young and following a challenging time in her life, I made the decision to be proactive with her mental health and advised her school she would be missing every other Friday. There was no discussion about it; I just made it happen. I told them her mental health was more important to me than her grades. The teachers understood my intentions and were supportive; the administration, not so much. I didn't care. This was my child, and I was going to raise her and care for her to the best of my ability. I can be stubborn like that, and I will fight for those who I love to the death, so you better be ready for a fight. Of course, it helps when you show up to the school wearing a uniform and carrying a side arm.

Every other weekend, I had three days off work. I worked hard, but I was raised to play harder. I wanted my daughter to learn how to be strong and independent, undefined by limitations others would want to put on her. So we would go camping. There is nothing like unpacking a trailer and creating a temporary home in the forest. Setting up a tent that was more inviting than any five-star resort could offer is an amazing feeling, collecting kindling and firewood for the evening fire where I've cooked everything from tacos to pizza. I took great pride in learning to cook under the canopy of evergreens surrounded by quizzical squirrels and blue jays. It was a whimsical wildness of peace, quiet, and serenity that my heart longs for even today.

The best part of our mental health days were the walks through the woods. The sound of our hiking boots pounding the footpaths along cliffs and alleys carved through the trees were only interrupted by discussions of the heart. Frequently, we would stop in our tracks and crouch down to observe bears and deer grazing nearby. We would read books that explained how Native Americans and early settlers explored the undisturbed wilderness and would wonder. We always took a camera to capture those trips, and they are my fond treasures that still today can take me back to a serene time shared with the most cherished person in my life. I can't wait to share some mental-health days with my grandchildren who are blessed to experience their own mental-health days with their mom and dad. I wish more moms and dads could find time to enjoy their children and create their own mental-health days. The memories would be well worth the effort.

Prepare

Long-established patterns are changing and these changes are creating for some anxiety over the unknown and depression for what is lost. When you know what to look for, you can recognize the shifts in the patterns and change your reactions to responses, your attitude toward change, and the consequences caused by the changes can be reduced. Conversely, when you don't recognize the patterns, you'll constantly find yourself reeling, falling, and quitting as you feel overwhelmed and afraid as you feel hopeless in light of all the changes.

I often tell my clients to step back and take a look at the patterns. Patterns are revealed over time when you find yourself feeling *stuck*. Consider these examples:

If you are arguing over the same problems that never get resolved, what is the pattern of solving the problems? Do you fight because no one has any solutions, and you both just keep pointing out the problems? Or are the solutions obvious, but no one wants to be responsible for making the change?

When neither person wants to be responsible for making change, no change can happen. In one way, this is comforting because with change, *someone* must be responsible for initiating, controlling, and continuing the change. They also are responsible for the success or failures of that change. This sounds risky to the person who wants to avoid responsibility, and so they want to push the responsibility onto the other person (spouse, partner, parent, or child).

All change is difficult. It gets real when you realize that the only way to make a change is for you to be responsible for that change.

Often, parents will bring their children in for therapy because *they* are depressed or anxious. After listening to the problems, I will often turn to the parent and inform them that this is not the child's problem to solve but theirs. Tears will fall, anger will flare up, and defensiveness usually gets directed at me, until they realize I'm speaking truth. They can kick the ground and stomp their feet, but ultimately, the choice is theirs if they want to help their child or only blame them. Sometimes, it's an easy fix that only requires tweaking what they currently are doing. More often, the parent has childhood trauma of their own that is being manifested in their current relationship with their child.

When we address the parent's childhood trauma, we can fix their current relationship problems with their own children. A willingness to do this is key to the success of change. A parent who refuses to take responsibility for changing their past will fail at effecting change in their present. You can't give what you don't have, and an unhealthy parent cannot help an unhealthy child without change. You will repeat unhealthy patterns from your childhood in your parenting style today, and you'll be stuck in an emotional time warp that can continue with your grandchildren as well. A hardened heart that refuses to investigate the past will not be able to look at the present.

Parenting is like soil that must be tilled prior to planting. This means it gets ripped up, flipped over, revealing any roots from prior plantings. Bringing the roots to the surface and letting them dry out creates a soil that is nourished and ready for the new seeds. When a parent refuses to till the soil before planting their own "seeds," their children are being choked out by their past roots. Tear out your old roots, and your children will grow to blossoming beauties.

> *As the heavens are higher than the earth,*
> *so are my ways higher than your ways*
> *and my thoughts than your thoughts.*
> *As the rain and the snow*
> *come down from heaven,*
> *and do not return to it*
> *without watering the earth*

and making it bud and flourish,
so that it yields seed for the sower and bread for the
eater,
so is my word that goes out from my mouth:
It will not return to me empty,
but will accomplish what I desire
and achieve the purpose for which I sent it.
You will go out in joy
and be led forth in peace;
the mountains and hills
will burst into song before you,
and all the trees of the field
will clap their hands. (Isaiah 55:9–12 NIV)

Technology

In the animal world there is a term called imprinting. This is when an animal can believe they are another species. A kitten can nurse right alongside puppies and think it is a dog. In much the same way, technology is negatively impacting babies and young children. Their undeveloped minds can be manipulated and molded so they have difficulty recognizing reality from fantasy. They have no ability to challenge a lie or distinguish what is true from fiction. Parents are ignorant of the flood of false information their children consume and then wonder, "Where do they come up with such nonsense?" When parents quit engaging with their children and give their children over to technology, children are the ones who suffer. Critical thinking is replaced by conformity, and conformity at all costs is turning children into robots. They are being programmed to believe lies, and the only way to save them is to turn off technology. You may say, "But they will fight me on this." Yes, yes, they will. With everything in their being, they want to be like everyone else. But if they were using cocaine or drinking a fifth of vodka in your presence, wouldn't you take those harmful things away from them? When parents understand that technology is more addictive than any drug, maybe they will be willing to save their child from the abuse of it.

Sometimes there's a question of what comes first, the chicken or the egg. I don't know the answer to that question, but I do know how it evolves when it comes to our children's self-esteem. As very young children, we learn our self-worth from our environment, our parents, and our extended family members. As we get older, we gain information about our self-worth through our peers, our teachers, and others who would have influence over us. As we reach adulthood, our relationships can exacerbate insecurities rooted from our childhood experiences.

Arguments can start because someone is "pushing our buttons," which means they're coming too close to the mark that reinforces our low self-worth. We crave affirmation and encouragement from our peers and seek to find our security in others. We give away our power because we are exchanging it for encouragement, validation, and affirmation that we are seen as a "good" person as we seek to have value in their eyes. Unfortunately, we are attracted to other people with similar low self-esteem because we fear being judged by those who have what we actually desire. We want to feel better about ourselves but don't know how.

Children today are doing more self-harm through cutting, drugs, alcohol, and suicide than ever before. They are screaming for attention, but their parents are not hearing their pleas because they are too distracted, tired, or busy to pay attention. At young ages, parents would give their children their phones to distract them long enough so the parents could get tasks done or just have a completed conversation on the phone. Parents did not know they were over-stimulating their young minds and creating neurological pathways that would later resemble ADHD, generalized anxiety, and depressive disorders. When parents try to take their children's phone away as a form of discipline, some children go into an uncontrollable rage. Fearful parents return the phones to their children rather than address the problem. They now have reinforced the bad behavior, and the child knows how to get what they want. Parents beg, plead, and cry for their children to change, but the children know they have all the power, and parents feel powerless to make any change.

The solution is consistency. Parents must agree on a plan of action and then stick to it. Flip-flopping back and forth on consequences or having only one form of discipline prevents options when necessary. If you give the phone as a reward and take it away as discipline, eventually, the discipline will not work, and the reward is meaningless. Take technology away from your children at night and put them on chargers in your room and out of their reach. Give it to them only when necessary. Every time you drive, you don't need a movie or a playlist to keep the kids distracted. Don't let them sleep with their phones. They don't sleep, and you are not monitoring their exposure to unhealthy content. For centuries, children went to school without a phone and were safe. If schools would secure phones at school or ban them altogether, students might receive better grades and may even pay attention to what is being taught.

Landmarks

We have lost sight of the landmarks that used to tell us where we are on our journey of life. Prepandemic, you went to school, and you knew there was a graduation day that marked the ending of the era of dependence, and you entered an area of independence. You knew you were going to get a job, go to college, move out of your parents' home. You made plans to enter the military or learn a trade. You might even have thought about traveling abroad to far-off lands or walking down the aisle with your high school sweetheart. Life was filled with ambition and hope for a bright future. But the pandemic stole all of that away from our youth, and another year of pandemic pandemonium is stealing hope from this year's graduates. No wonder they are all depressed and feeling hopeless. Consider the loss of these landmark moments:

- No graduation day
- No prom night
- No college campus acceptance (only online)
- No job security
- No wedding without masks and proof of vaccine

- No travel abroad
- No apartments available or affordable
- No independence as forced to live at home
- No individuating as they are forced to remain under parental authority

So what can they do? They can create opportunity to set mile markers in their lives. They can prepare now for when the doors get unlocked, and the chains of authoritarian decision-making is lifted. They can plan for their future in the present and celebrate the successes they make today. Parents need to help their children learn how to become adults. Unfortunately, most parents today have never learned these life lessons. Adulting doesn't just happen. You might get older, but you may not be "growing up." There are lessons you can learn now that will prevent you from the trial and errors of traditional transitioning when leaving the home.

Here are some ways to focus on the planning stages of life:

1. *Make a plan.* Write down everything you hope to achieve for the next year. If you plan to go to college, travel, get married, move out, write it down. The new year is a great place to execute a plan.

2. *Research.* If you plan to move out of your parent's home and into an apartment, look at the price of renting an apartment. Remember, most apartments and property managements have requirements before you can even qualify to rent a space (credit report, employment, tax return, three months' rent). If you do not have these things established, it's time to get to it. If you hope to get married, check which venues are open, their restrictions, costs, and limitations to guest numbers. Prices have skyrocketed as many venues closed due to the pandemic, and supply and demand raises costs. If you plan to go to college, even the simple application and acceptance process has changed. Financial aid, housing restrictions, and access to services have all been negatively affected by the pandemic.

3. *Create a budget.* What good does it do to have a dream if you can't afford it? Everyone is learning to live with less and less as prices soar, and inflation creeps into our wallets, shrinking our bank accounts. If Mom and Dad have been your banker, it's time to find your own means of support. There is no more ability to spend your way to happiness. You must save what you can, and *before* you move out is the best time to do it.

4. *Compromise.* There is a saying, "Shoot for the stars; even if you miss, you might just land on the moon." It's great to have ambitious goals, but they must be realistic and attainable. Look for ways to get near your dreams: If you want to travel, work for a nonprofit that travels to where you want to go. If you want a big expensive wedding but don't have the financial means, see how you can cut costs. If you want an apartment at the beach, look for a room to rent or roommates to share the cost so you don't have to it alone.

When you consider how you can start planning for your future, optimism may replace discouragement, and proactive intention might replace contemplation stagnation.

Tenacity

Have you ever watched two dogs size each other up before the dogfight begins? They circle, sniff, and measure their weight against the challenge before them. But what you can't see is their self-confidence, degree of courage, or know how many previous dogfights they've won. Often, it's not the size of the dog in the fight that will determine the winner but the size of the fight that determines who wins. Success is like that.

Where do you see success in your life? What is the tool that measures your success? Do you compare yourself to others? And whether you are doing a little bit better financially or have a bigger home or have a better-looking family. Does this mean success? Conversely, do you compare and see yourself as a failure? Do you look only at the challenge and see it as bigger than you and quit before you have a chance to win? Or are you tenacious, unrelenting, and determined beyond reasoning? Do you choose to enter the fight knowing you risk everything, even while knowing the odds of winning are stacked against you? If you only measure your successes by your failures, then how will you ever know what true success is?

The definition of *tenacity* (Oxford University): "The quality or fact of being able to grip something firmly or being determined. The quality or fact of continuing to exist. Persistence." Life is filled with challenges, and you may be in the fight of your life. Not everything you value is worth fighting for. I wouldn't fight for *things*, but I will fight to the death to protect family and those I love. We strive to hold on to that which we know and love, the familiar, the comforts of the past, people, places, and things. We place a high value on people and experiences that have brought meaning to an otherwise meaningless life. And we desire to keep them safe for all time.

If we are not paying attention, we can become distracted and not be as tenacious as we once were. We can struggle to regain our grip, only to find our grip has gone weak, and over time we can lose hold of the things we held most precious. We also can be vulnerable to those who would rip from us that which we value most. Parents who have been asleep at the wheel are now waking to find someone else is at the wheel, and that person is driving their children toward destruction. Now that they are awake, parents are determined to get back in the driver's seat and regain control and protect their children from harm. They have chosen to be tenacious and persistent, and they are confident the fight will be won.

There are two worlds at war, and the ones fighting are suffering in a battle not of their making. Parents, for too long, have been unaware that their children are depressed and anxious. When I heard social media went offline, my first reaction was, "Thank God!" I think social media is creating conflict, dividing our nation, promoting hate crimes, and is supporting crimes against humanity. When I saw an increase of parents bringing children in for mental health services, I thought, "Thank God!"

When I heard workers were pushing back against the unfair treatment they were receiving from their employers, I thought, "Thank God!" I have been wondering where the American spirit has been, and now I see American ingenuity is rising to the occasion and solutions are bubbling to the surface.

I learned a long time ago that the fall of the Roman Empire was caused by the destruction of the family. The family unit has been under attack for decades, and one positive that came from the school shutdowns and business lockdowns was families were forced to spend time together. Suddenly, they saw what the children were doing on their phones all day, they saw who their friends were, they saw the social media content they were addicted to, and they realized their children were addicted to porn, vaping, and self-harm. Parents are arming up to fight for their children's lives, their future, and it looks like momma and poppa bears around the globe are saying, "Not my child!" What a great example they are being to their children who have been wanting parents to stand up for them and protect them. Children are being blessed by parents who are showing them they care, that their families come first, and that the parents will fight tooth and nail for righteousness' sake. If you want to see your child's mental health improve, *you* need to learn how to be a parent first. The children are not the problem; poor parenting is the problem. The school is not the problem; poor parenting is the problem. The political climate is not the problem; poor parenting is the problem. Society isn't the problem; again poor parenting is the problem. If you don't know how to be a parent first and foremost, learn. Good parenting is a skill anyone can learn. It's not too late to learn. Start today, and you will be helping your children have a better tomorrow. Tomorrow's legacy is being built by your decisions today. The battles won are the victories remembered.

Be careful! Watch and pray. You do not know
when it will happen. (Mark 13:33 NLV)

CHAPTER 12

Intentional Leadership

*Enter through the narrow gate. For wide is
the gate and broad is the road that leads to
destruction, and many enter through it.*
> —Matthew 7:13 (NLV)

We have a leadership crisis. Men are not leading their families and are abandoning mothers and children to fend for themselves. Employers are forcing their most impoverished employees into unemployment over forced vaccine mandates. Our children are suffering as they are pulled back and forth with the tides of change. And our veterans suffer the consequences of a world at war. Livelihoods are being stolen as taxes, gas, and food prices climb higher and higher, and when we look for solutions from our leadership, we discover they are the ones creating the problems. As a mental health provider, it's difficult to listen day in and day out to the flood of fear and pain resulting from the unending waves of change.

I am a simple thinker. I look at a problem and try to solve it in a simple manner. Complexity only prolongs the suffering for the client and results in higher costs: emotional, physical, spiritual, and financial. There is a term called intestinal fortitude, which means that someone can stomach a difficult situation because they possess courage, fearlessness, and have a heart that is rooted in valor and virtue. They are the ones going through the challenge or difficulty.

We need leaders who embrace these qualities, not leaders who stand on the sideline watching someone else suffer. There is no courage in that, only cowardliness.

For decades, America has been asking, where are the leaders? Who can we trust? Where is the help? I wish there was an 800-What-The-Heck phone number we could dial and complain. But alas, no one is picking up the calls. There's no funding for it. The issues that face America did not start because of the pandemic. For some time now, we have turned our attention away from the ills of society in the name of tolerance. Homelessness has increased exponentially, domestic violence is skyrocketing, drug addiction and alcohol abuse is a pandemic unto itself, unemployment continues to increase, crime is out of control, the number of suicides and murders are uncontrolled, and all the while, accountability decreases. I believe we have a shortage of true leaders whose actions are consistent with their words. In other words, there are a whole lot of people who are looking for leaders to stand up for what is right and what is true and who can create a pathway others can follow. Leadership cannot happen haphazardly by reacting to situations. Leadership must be intentional, designed for success, developed with a strategic plan, and the courage to execute that plan. Preparation and execution will determine a successful outcome, or it won't.

Déjà vus

Most of the time, this pattern has been repeated throughout history. What we are seeing has been seen before. The war we are fighting has been fought and won. The challenges of today will spark a revival of the spirit, and one day soon, I believe truth will prevail, love will win over hate, and law and order will once again rule the land. In his letter titled "The Crisis" (1776), Thomas Pain wrote about the tyranny that was fought during the battle against the British and the reasons that stirred a nation to war.

> *Were government a mere manufacture or*
> *article of commerce immaterial by whom it should*

be made or sold, we might as well employ her as another, but when we consider it as the foundation from whence the general manners and morality of a country take their rise, that the persons entrusted with the execution thereof are by their serious example an authority to support these principles, how abominably absurd is the idea of being hereafter governed by a set of men who have been guilty of forgery, perjury, treachery, theft, and every species of villainy which the lowest wretches on earth could practice or invent.

We have turned into a society of complainers, and we need a society of doers to rise up. If you don't agree with something you have no control over, stop trying to change it and change you. If you're unhappy with what is happening to you, your family, your job, your finances, then decide for personal change. Establish your boundaries and expectations. What are you not willing to tolerate? Ask yourself what you want, look at your options, and then determine how you will change your circumstances. When you sit in a car with someone else behind the wheel, and they refuse to take you where you want to go, pounding your fist on the dashboard and screaming at them doesn't help. Maybe you need to take the wheel or get out of the car altogether. When change is required, most often, the one needing to change is the one doing the most complaining.

Home

Intentional leadership happens inside your home and everywhere outside of it. The legacy you give to your children and their children's children is birthed in your leadership skills as a parent. I grew up reading and watching Winnie-the-Pooh and Christopher Robin in the Hundred Acre Wood. The wisdom of Winnie was put into written format, drawn on paper, illustrated in Saturday morning cartoons, and made for films *on the big screen*. I cut my teeth on the corners of *The Complete Tales of Winnie the Pooh*. In elementary school, my nickname was Tigger, and I embraced the image of Tigger because I truly was "fun, fun, fun!"

The essence of my life has been shaped by many things, but the one thing that I hold on to the most is my desire to be loved, not only loved but to be accepted for all of my qualities—good, bad, beautiful, and yes, even the ugly parts, because this is where wisdom is found. One gift of age is wisdom, but wisdom is not measured in years but in tears.

Sometimes, life can make us feel like we're drowning in a cesspool of regret. Negative memories of past behaviors and subsequent consequences float around in our brains, and they all cause pain. Keeping afloat in those dark waters becomes our only focus as we paddle, kick, and splash about in an effort to keep our mouth and nose out of the sewage. Exhausted and alone, life can get pretty messy, and depression can begin to encroach in as discouragement and hopelessness increases. Turning off these truthful remembrances is difficult, and the guilt and shame of the past can keep us frozen and unable to live our life in the moment. The challenge is to focus on the blessings we have today and to live in the presence of joy.

As I've gotten older and moved into a season of grandmotherhood, the wisdom I gained from Pooh-Bear speaks to my heart even more. This cartoon character spoke so loudly to my heart as I read Piglet asking Winnie-the-Pooh, "Pooh, promise you won't forget about me, ever. Not even when I'm a hundred." I listen to older men and women (my age and older) share how they are alone, and they fear growing even older all alone. Some share their regrets and how their choices in their youth led to words and actions they wish they now could take back. Those choices resulted in their children not speaking with them and how they reject any effort to connect. These people who have come to therapy to find solutions and ways of reconnecting are crushed when they learn that they have no control over their children's choices. I explain that they can only change their own choices and make better choices for themselves. I encourage them that as they change, their children may recognize over time that they are not the same person and may become open to reconciliation. Ultimately, everyone has a right to choose who they want to be in a relationship with. We all want to be accepted. Try loving and accepting the person whom you have wronged even while they are being unloving to you. Say to yourself, "A legacy of love has become my focus, and my purpose is to share it with everyone." The past does not define your present situation, and by becoming a better person, you just might influence others to see a change in you.

Strength

Have you noticed how angry you've become lately? Do you feel like you want to run away but don't know where to go? Do you pace in your mind and roll over in your bed, restless and irritable, searching for the cause of your agitation? Do you watch the news looking for information that could help you figure out what is wrong in the world, searching for solutions that will give you some peace? All this negative energy is actually very easy to explain.

The problem: brokenness.

The solution: strength.

Brokenness begins at birth. Abuse experienced as a child doesn't have to be physical or sexual to be emotionally traumatic. A child born into a home where boundaries are broken, anger is openly expressed, and fear prevails will experience brokenness. The brokenness experienced as a child remains brokenness as an adult. We live in a world filled with broken people who hurt each other. We hurt the ones we love, and we hurt those who oppose us. We hurt ourselves. We hurt inwardly with depression, and we hurt those nearby with anger. We all hurt. Brokenness manifests as hate, selfishness, and greed. These are foolish attempts to feel strong. Brokenness keeps us focused on ourselves, and that makes us weak.

The opposite of brokenness is strength, but what is strength, and where does it come from? When I ask individuals and couples this question, they have difficulty coming up with an answer. They flounder and compare strength with courage or wisdom or physical dexterity. Strength comes from intent—intentionally resisting the things that cause hurt. When we intentionally focus our lives on kindness, generosity, and love, we come from a place of strength, and that strength overcomes our brokenness. The more intentional we are, the stronger we become. The stronger we become, the less broken we are. The less broken we are, the better choices we make. If you want to live strong, live intentionally.

When I was enrolled in my master's program, I took a personality test. The results of that test indicated that I experience justice in a very black-and-white way. One hundred percent of my belief is that there is justice and injustice in this world. Which side of the equation you live by is determined by your desire to live according to the law, not the laws men create but the laws created by God. When you ignore the laws created by man, you can receive one of several punishments. You may be fined, imprisoned, or even lose your life. If you ignore God's laws, you may also lose liberty unto death—but death eternal. God's law is rooted in truth, and that truth will remain long after we are gone. It is God's legacy. We who believe in God's law also live in his truth. It is in his truth that we can find strength to face the uncertainty of the world. It is where we can stand firm against tyranny and injustice and fight against the evil intentions of others. God's truth is found in the tears of a mother who stands over her children to protect them. It's found in the scars of the father who stands in harm's way for his family. It is the strength of the individual who fights for their rights, and it is found in the few who fight against the many.

Retirement

What do you do when you don't know what to do but know you must do something? Imagine you have been given an instruction book to your life, and when you open the book, the pages are all blank. That is what it is like for our men and women leaving a career of service. Service jobs include the military, but it also means those who have retired from law enforcement, firefighters, doctors, and nurses. It's the career secretary, teacher, waitress, and cook. It's the business owner who closes shop, transfers ownership, or hands the business over to a loved one. The impact of leaving a career that you've been dedicated to for decades can be exciting and terrifying at the same time.

The day after retirement, you awaken to the alarm you forgot to turn off. You lay there in bed thinking how blissful it is not to have to answer to that annoyance ever again and softly fall back to sleep. Minutes later, you awaken and lay there wondering what you should do today. Every routine you've gotten used to performing has disappeared overnight, and you must create new patterns of behavior, new routines, set new goals, and find new ways to fill the day. It's amazing how much time there is when you have nothing to do except notice how much time you have. If you don't write something down in the blank pages of your book, you will fill the days with boredom and useless endeavors that bring little to no joy. Regret and resentment will begin to weigh on you as you look around at the unprepared future with fear, frustration, and confusion.

I have seen an increase of individuals coming to therapy to try to understand the cause of their anxious thoughts and emotional lows. What they had been looking forward to for so many years with giddy anticipation has turned out to be nothing like what they had planned. The travel plans have disappeared as COVID restrictions linger, and the costs of travel soar. When the reality that they were happier working in a job that made them miserable settles in, they feel defeated.

So I take them by the hand and show them a life they get to create! We look at the possibilities, passions, and hobbies they might still enjoy. We look at what brought them joy while they worked, but they never had enough time to do it. We look at discount travel and modes of transportation not considered. We talk about a home oasis versus as total remodel. It's amazing how good you feel when you declutter your home office, your closet, and your garage. Investing in new shelving, painting the walls, and upgrading with new lamps and rugs can do a complete refresh to a familiar area. New bedding in the bedroom also is an inexpensive way to brighten up your space. One benefit of retirement is you get to pick a part-time job that gives you joy. If you enjoy golf, bowling, or sipping Starbucks, see if they have any openings and work as little or as much as you want.

The money you earn will pay for your hobbies in your off time. If you enjoy crafting, try applying at Hobby Lobby for the holiday. If you find sewing or home decor interesting, apply to work in a furniture store or Joanna's. Employers need experienced workers with a foundational work ethic. You can pretty much ask for your preferred hours and even your preference in pay. Even if it's not comparable to your prior job, it doesn't matter. You're there for the joy of it now, and joy you will find. If you don't like it, do something else. The world is your oyster, and the buffet of life is before you. Sample everything, do what you like, and enjoy the journey.

When you look around at all that is wrong, it can be overwhelming. But when you look with fresh eyes at all the possibilities, you can feel encouraged and reenergized. When you look at each day as a gift from God, you can receive the blessings he freely gives you. If you focus on the past and what you don't have, you will miss the good times you could be making today. Remember, you are a leader even if the only one following is you!

Erick H. Erickson, a prominent psychologist of the twentieth century, said, "Healthy children will not fear life if their elders have integrity enough not to fear death." In other words, we must live intentionally, even in the process of dying. If we are living only for ourselves, then we end up dying alone—with ourselves. It's only through forfeiting our own selfish ambitions that we can learn to truly live a life that is fulfilling and purposeful. This doesn't just happen. We have a lot to lose when we give away a life that we designed for our own selfish endeavors. We must relinquish an identity rooted in our individual abilities, gifts, and talents. Everything we know must be stripped from us leaving us naked, vulnerable, and fearful. When everything you know to be true is shown to be a lie, it is terrifying. Deception cuts to the core of our being and can leave us deeply wounded. When we realize it's not because of our own strength but God's strength living in us, we can rise above the ashes and move forward to a life that has been designed with a purpose. A life formulated not by our own hands but by the hands of our Creator is much better than a life we can create on our own.

The amazing thing about realizing your life purpose is that you quickly realize your life is not all about you. You are a vessel God uses to help others. If you were a cup, *he* would pour his life into you, and you would provide his living water to others who are thirsting for God's righteousness. The more you give away, the larger the vessel God gives you, which enables you to give even more. When you bless others, you make room for more of God's blessings. When you pour out God's love to your family, friends, neighbors, coworkers, and strangers, be ready because God will smile down on you as he pours out more blessings on your head.

The Bible says, "There is no greater love than to lay down one's life for one's friends" (John 15:13). Only through our sacrifices will we earn treasures in heaven. What we accomplish here on earth is only limited by the time that we are here on earth. Everything tangible (money, fame, success) will have lost meaning and disappear after we are gone. But when we build up our treasures in heaven, they will live in eternity. Our legacy is our final report card determined by how well we lived, good or bad, and it will exist forever unchanged.

I love and fear the term *eternal praise*. It conjures up in my mind that how I lived, the people I influenced, the legacy I leave behind will live on into eternity. Our legacy, good or bad, will be the result of our intentionality or failure of it. We can blindly walk through a life where wisdom has eluded us, leaving a trail of foolish consequences behind us. Relationship carnage can be scattered on the pathways of our lives where the innocent suffered more harm than received our love. So I repeat myself because I feel it is worthy of repeating: We must live intentional, even in the process of dying.

> *For the Spirit God gave us does not make us timid, but gives us power, love and self-discipline.* (2 Timothy 1:7 NLV)

CHAPTER 13

Intentional Grace

For it is by grace you have been saved, through faith—
and this is not from yourselves, it is the gift of God.
                                        —Ephesians 2:8 (NLV)

Grace is the ultimate gift of forgiveness one can give another. We all need to learn to be givers of grace, and so often, we don't even know how. In the days of old, *grace* was another word for clemency, or when a judge would not enforce a penalty a criminal deserved. The accused would throw himself on the mercy of the court and hope the judge would show them grace by reducing their sentence or letting them off with a strong warning. When someone has done us harm, we can also show them grace through the process of forgiveness.

Forgiveness has three parts:

- I forgive you because I want to reconcile.
- I forgive you and give you over to God.
- I forgive myself.

In the first instance I may know the person who has wounded me. They may be my family member, spouse, or friend. The offense may be one that caused hurt feelings but not so bad that I don't want them in my life. I still want the relationship and I'm willing to take steps to repair the damage. And forgiveness is a bridge to make that happen. I may tell them how they offended me, receive an apology, and forgive them. We may have a discussion that brings clarity, sets boundaries, and establishes expectations to avoid any future offense. Both parties participated, and reconciliation is possible.

In the second type of forgiveness, the wounded person must forgive even if they do not hear an apology from the other party. This forgiveness is necessary to stop the offense from causing further damage to the victim. The offense may be so egregious that the victim does not want to continue a relationship with the offender (as in cases of adultery, abuse, or deception) and must forgive the offender in order to gain closure. They may not know the offender as in the case of an aggravated assault, rape, or other abuse. There may or may not be a criminal trial. The victim needs to forgive the offender and give them over to God for justice.

In the third type of forgiveness, the wounded must forgive themselves for any part of the offense. They may have had harsh words with a loved one and condemn themselves for their bad behavior. They may have been drinking and driving which resulted in the injury of another. They may have committed any number of offenses against one or more people. Or they may silently isolate in guilt and shame for a crime they've not committed but for which they take full responsibility. Sometimes this type of forgiveness is the hardest to accept because we know how bad we feel, know the sinfulness of our actions, and fear the judgment from others, so we judge ourselves more harshly than anyone else ever could.

Carrie (not her real name) was a woman in her sixties who had two daughters. One she said was "perfect," and the other was the "screw up." The first daughter created no problems for her as a mother, and Carrie felt her success as a parent was reflected in the successes of her perfect daughter. But when she looked at the failings of her second daughter, she reacted in anger, withdrew her love, and set harsh rules and boundaries. Carrie expressed a need to deal with her depression which she blamed on her daughter's many failings that included drugs, prison, and three children Carrie was now raising. Even as tears fell from her eyes, she felt justified to be angry and didn't feel it was her responsibility to be kind. Carrie couldn't see that her depression was rooted in her unwillingness to forgive her daughter, but it also stemmed from her unwillingness to forgive herself.

When Keena (not her real name) walked through my office the first time we met, she wore a hoodie sweatshirt and dark sunglasses. When she revealed who she saw herself as, she screamed, "I'm Freddie Krueger." She had been severely burnt in an accident while cooking with hot grease. One day while making breakfast for her three young children, she accidentally bumped the frying pan and flipped the hot grease onto her face and upper torso. The visit to the burn ward for third-degree burns, subsequent surgeries, and separation from her children were nothing compared to the pain she felt when her parents filed a Child Protective Services (CPS) report saying she was an unfit mother and said the accident occurred because Keena was under the influence for illegal drugs. The truth was that Keena had been recently gang raped and was prescribed antidepressants that made her groggy and unstable. The injustice she felt made her angry at the world for the many wrongs she had suffered as a child and young woman. Now at the age of fifty, she was finally seeking help.

Sancho (not his real name) entered my office so angry at his employer he was threatening suicide. He said he was being wrongfully charged with false allegations of sexual misconduct that threatened his retirement and the possibility of imprisonment if he was found guilty. Sancho was so angry at the untruth he was willing to die on principle. He knew he was innocent but was angry that his character was being attacked by his employer on a job where he had worked for the past eighteen years.

In all these situations, there is justification for anger, frustration, and a desire for revenge. When truth is being ignored, when we are forced to suffer the consequence for other people's choices, it's very easy to get stuck in a state of mind that keeps us looking for justice and retribution. In most cases, we never receive the sentence of "innocent," and seldom is justice serviced or retribution administered to our satisfaction.

These examples are extreme, and most people will not face such difficulties. Most people will find themselves fighting anxiety and depression over injustices with their family (spouse, partner, children, or parents), work, or friendships. They don't understand when someone has done them wrong (intentionally or otherwise), the other is not fixated on making the situation *right*. They also feel *justified* in what they did, and so the two find themselves at a stalemate of righteous indignation where both sides of the debate are unwavering. Sometimes, you must give up the need for justice so you can move on and live a life free of negative emotions. When you hold on to the past, injustice can turn you into a negative, argumentative, defensive, confrontational, unlovable, albeit justified *victim*. Sometimes, like in the case of Sancho, we need to prove our innocence so much we are willing to kill ourselves to punish someone who has hurt us. We can isolate in depression, feeling sad that no one notices. We can cut our arms and legs hoping someone will see our pain. We can drink ourselves to oblivion hoping the one who hurt us will bring us back to life. But none of these things will change our circumstances for long. We must change if we want to see real change, and that change begins with grace.

Most people don't know or care how you feel. Once they have harmed you, they have moved on to harming others. They are not watching you as you hurt yourself, fall into depression, or experience panic attacks. They may look at your self-destructive behaviors as further evidence that they were justified in their actions. I show my clients that if they really want the truth to be known, live it. If they want justice to be served, give up the need for it. If they want retribution, let your joy and personal successes shine bright. This way, you'll be living the best life that you have intentionally created and have overcome the injustices of your past.

When Carrie understood that she was still judging her daughter's youth and refusing to see the efforts she made as a forty-year-old woman, she was able to let go of the need for retribution. When she realized she was judging her success as a parent by her daughter's failures, she was able to forgive herself and reconcile with her daughter.

When Keena could learn to love herself and returned to dancing (she was a professional performer), her self-confidence returned, and she was able to confront her parents, gain clarity, and understanding.

They had not known she was under a doctor's care. She was able to forgive her past and live her best life in the present.

When Sancho realized his suicidal thoughts were rooted in his need for approval and to be seen by others as perfect, he was able to let go of that need and live according to his character. When he saw that his suicidal thoughts made him appear guilty, he became determined to live by his knowledge of the truth. Sancho was able to give himself grace, and he found the inner strength to fight. He turned his anger and frustration toward exposing the truth, and truth prevailed. All charges were dropped, and he returned to work vindicated. When he forgave himself and lived true to his character, others were able to see the truth in all things.

Grace is necessary to live an intentional life. *Grace* is mentioned 138 times in the Bible and is considered the most important concept. It is because of God's love for us that we receive his grace and mercy, and we are instructed to love and give grace to others. We must accept our own imperfections and forgive the flaws of others. We cannot lead others with confidence if we are looking in the rear mirror at our mistakes and regrets. We must make choices through a growth mindset that requires grace to grow. Our character, including our ability to be humble, insists that we can't be humble while we lack grace. We must be present in our mistakes as well as our victories, make choices that include grace, and we must love always with a heart filled with grace. Successful relationships, communication, and even finances require grace, and parents and leaders need grace in order to continue to lead.

When I talk with my patients about forgiveness, I use an analogy of driving a car with the windshield blacked out, and they are trying to drive by looking in their rear mirror only. When I ask them how well they think they would reach their desired destination, they admit it would seem nearly impossible without some assistance or guidance. I explain this is how they drive their life, blindly making decisions that end in a crash. When they are focused on the mistakes of their past, on regrets, shame, and guilt that they cannot change, for events they cannot alter, they are driving looking in the rear mirror.

I show them how to rip the rear mirror completely off their dirty windshield and begin to focus on cleaning up the mess so they can see. Gradually, they wipe away the distractions, the blind spots, and smudges, and eventually, the path is made clear. When they have a clear of their destination, they begin to make decisions that lead them in their desired direction. The more clarity, the faster they can go, and the momentum increases as they race toward the goal.

As in all situations where intention or distraction determines outcomes, intentionality wins out every time. Even if you find yourself off course, you know how you got there because even getting lost was done with intention. I believe Mark Twain said it best when he talked about death and living, "The fear of death follows from the fear of life. A man who lives fully is prepared to die at any time."

For to me, to live is Christ and to die is gain.
(Philippians 1:21 NLV)

CHAPTER 14

Final Thoughts

I will instruct you and teach you in the way you should
go; I will counsel you with my loving eye on you.
—Psalm 3:28 (NLV)

How you define yourself is more important than how others define you. The challenge to change what you believe about yourself is often the main focus of therapy. Every time we are deceived, wounded, harmed, and recover, there is a tendency to minimize the effects of the pain. This minimizing happens in cases of child abuse, domestic violence, and rape. It also happens in cases of racism and discrimination. It is part of our humanity to intuitively desire change. Some people bounce back after someone has hurt them, while others slowly regain footing. Still some will never recover completely and will suffer silently, fearing they are a burden to others who tell them to "move on." These individuals have the desire to change but not the knowledge and this book was written for them.

When I was eleven years old, I knew I wanted to follow in my older brother's footsteps and become a police officer. For twenty-five years, I served as a deputy sheriff in Los Angeles County. In 2005, I was forced to retire at the rank of sergeant when I was injured on the job. I was terrified to learn my income would be cut in half due to my disabilities. I was a single mom with a teenage daughter and was in fear of losing my home. My faith was all I had, and God was there for me every step of the way.

In 2006, I went back to school, and in four years, I completed both my bachelor's and master's degrees in psychology and marriage and family therapy. It wasn't easy as I was the oldest in my class, worked two jobs, and still had to find time for my daughter. I passed my board exams and received my license on November 4, 2014, and opened my first counseling office twelve days later on November 16, 2014.

When I founded Encouragers Counseling & Training Centers Inc., a 501(c)(3) nonprofit organization, few decisions along the way were done without intention. I had two considerations that were my focused intent for my business: that it would always honor God, and that it would strive for excellence. The scripture above is on my business cards. The company logo my daughter created has the cross on a hill in the center of a shield (Ephesians 6:16). The mission statement is threefold:

- Excellence in service
- Excellence in training
- Excellence in business development

Not every decision I made was a good one, and many people have come and gone. Even though the journey after ten years has gone by so quickly, I have tried to follow my own advice by living intentionally.

Finally, know that I pray for you every day. I encourage you to make the decision to change. Plan for tomorrow but live for today. Live with hope, finding a reason to get out of bed every day. Make yourself a priority and give to yourself as much attention as you give to others. Spend time with yourself, getting to know what you like and dislike, and ultimately come to love yourself. When you realize that you don't have to dim yourself in order to let other people shine, that every opportunity to fail is seen as an opportunity for growth, you have found the first step to living intentional.

I pray that you have found this book useful and encouraging. If you would like to learn more about living an intentional life, go to our website and download our free activities booklet at EncouragersUSA. org. I pray you also may learn how to help yourself live the life you always wanted but never believed you could. Always chose to *live intentional.*

ABOUT THE AUTHOR

Vicki Coffman lived a life that was not always perfect, but it was intentional. At the age of eleven, Vicki knew she wanted to go into law enforcement as a career. After twenty-five years of service as a deputy sheriff, in 2005, she was forced into an early retirement following a job-related injury. She returned to school and received a master's degree and November 4, 2014, received her credentialing as a License Marriage and Family Therapist. Vicki founded a nonprofit called *Encouragers Counseling & Training Centers* and opened the doors to the practice November 16, 2014. Today, Vicki has founded a second professional counseling business called *Encouragers Family Counseling* and has offices in Southern California, Washington, and Virginia. *Live Intentional: Live the Life You Always Wanted but Never Believed You Could* is Vicki's first publication, with the *Live Intentional Workbook* and *Live Intentional 365 Daily Devotional* following close behind. Vicki believes there is a shortage of intentionality in the world. Those who have a plan to get where they want to go will most likely be the ones to arrive there.

If you'd like to learn more about Vicki and her work, find free downloads, or donate on her website, go to *EncouragersUSA.org*.

www.ingramcontent.com/pod-product-compliance
Lightning Source LLC
Chambersburg PA
CBHW031407150726
47989CB00002B/573